Living Without Electricity

Living Without Electricity

Stephen Scott
and Kenneth Pellman

People's Place Book #9

Good Books

Intercourse, PA 17534
800/762-7171

Acknowledgments
Photo Credits

Cover: front—Dick Brown; back—Blair Seitz. Beth Oberholtzer: 5, 38, 66, 93, 94, 111, 118, 121; Dick Brown: 7, 21, 23, 30 (right), 82-83, 113, 119; Mel Liechty: 8, 65 (bottom); Bernd Längin: 10, 127; John Zielinski: 12, 58, 120; Joan Liffring Zug: 19, 57 (bottom); Peter Gail/Goosefoot Acres: 22 (both), 30 (left), 31, 33, 35, 43, 50, 57 (upper right), 65 (top), 67, 74, 91 (top), 92, 117, 128, 137; Kenneth Pellman: 32, 46, 48, 57 (upper left); Stephen Scott: 34, 49, 100, 101 (both), 103, 136, 140, 146; Loren Berridge: 37; Patricia Fife/*Youngstown Vindicator*: 44; Jerry Irwin: 73, 145; Fred Wilson: 81 (top); Jeff Sprang: 81 (bottom), 110, 114; Richard Reinhold: 84, 102; Gene Puskar: 85, 91 (bottom); *Geauga Times Leader*: 135; Daniel Price: 141, 142; David Hunsberger: 143; Ignacio Gurruchaga/*Gente*: 148; Abe Warkentin: 149; Grace Goulder Izant/Hudson Public Library: 152.

Design by Dawn J. Ranck

LIVING WITHOUT ELECTRICITY
Copyright © 1990, 1999 by Good Books, Intercourse, PA 17534
First published in 1990
REVISED EDITION, 1999.
International Standard Book Number: 0-934672-61-X, paperback
International Standard Book Number: 1-56148-291-9, hardcover
Library of Congress Catalog Card Number: 89-49646

Library of Congress Cataloging-in-Publication Data
Scott, Stephen.
    Living without electricity / Stephen Scott and Kenneth
        Pellman. P. Cm.—(A People's Place book; no. 9)
    Includes bibliographical references.
    ISBN 0-934672-61-X, paperback; 1-56148-291-9, hardcover
    1. Amish—Social life and customs. 2. Electricity—Religious
aspects—Amish. I. Pellman, Kenneth, 1952- . II. Title. III. Series
E184.M45S36   1990
289.7'3—dc20   89-49646
                                                    CIP

Table of Contents

1.
Why Not Electricity?

Most North Americans today would think it impossible to do without electricity. Indeed, for people throughout the industrialized world, the most basic of life's activities rely upon through-the-wires power. Lighting, cooking, heating, grooming, and entertainment—all require volts and watts.

But electricity is actually a very recent development. While electrical power was available to many city dwellers in the early 1900s, the majority of rural North Americans had no access to current until the 1930s or 40s. Many people who were alive during the first third of this century will be able to identify with the accounts of Amish life in this book. Of course, to millions of people in the non-industrial nations, even the ways of the Amish may seem modern and luxurious.

A Connection With the World

What makes the Old Order Amish unique is not that they get along without electricity, but that they choose to do without it when it would be readily available. Most Amish see a link with electric wires as a connection with the world—the world that the Bible tells them they are to be "strangers and pilgrims" in.

Unlike many North Americans, the Amish value simplicity and self-denial over comfort, convenience, and leisure. So they try to discern the long-range effects of an innovation before deciding whether to adopt it.

An Amish home stands visibly apart from the outside world. There are no power lines, telephone lines, or television antennas.

Early in this century, the large majority of Amish leaders agreed that connecting to power lines would not be in the best interest of their communities. They did not make this decision because they thought electricity was evil in itself, but because easy access to it could lead to many temptations and the deterioration of church and family life. For similar reasons, the Amish refuse to own cars.

Forbidding electricity has prevented the need to make decisions on individual electrical devises, especially those used for entertainment. Radio and television promote values that are directly opposed to those of the Amish. These influences cannot easily come into the home if the usual door of entrance is not present.

Batteries and Generators

While rejecting TV and through-the-wires power, however, most Amish communities have accepted some use of battery-powered devices. All but the most conservative groups permit battery-operated clocks, watches, and flashlights. Calculators, electric shavers, and buggy lights that are powered by batteries are in wide use among the Amish, as are battery-operated electric fences which keep livestock from straying. In some areas, Amish dairy farmers have complied with milk company demands that they use battery-powered agitators in bulk milk tanks. Some Amish use solar generators to recharge these batteries.

In certain cases, electric generators may be used to operate equipment. Carpenters in some communities use portable generators to run their power tools, and many shops are equipped with welders operated by generators. Gasoline-powered generators are often used to charge 12-volt batteries. Occasionally, these batteries are connected to electric inverters to produce 100-volt current. Some Amish church districts allow businesses to run cash registers and typewriters in this way.

Most Amish believe that the number of devices that can be operated by a battery or generator is limited, and that careful use of such items poses minimal risk to community values. Moreover, these devices do not require a link to the outside world. Nevertheless, some Amish have tried to avoid even battery-powered items.

At the other end of the spectrum, a small minority of Amish have hooked into electrical power lines. These progressive Amish may still be considered Old Order because they use horse-drawn vehicles and have preserved traditional forms of worship and dress. Even these groups, however, restrict electrical use. The Amish community at Guthrie, Kentucky, for example, allows electricity but does not permit air conditioners or dishwashers. None of these groups allows members to have radios or TVs.

Do the Amish Change?

It one expects the Amish to be a living museum—a kind of religious Williamsburg, Virginia—then many Amish practices will seem inconsistent. Those who accuse the Amish of hypocrisy, however, fail to understand the goals of the community.

The ultra-conservative "White-Top," or "Nebraska," Amish of central Pennsylvania have allowed gasoline and diesel engines, but not self-propelled tractors.

Contrary to many popular accounts, the Amish do not oppose change. Members realize that they live differently from their 17th century ancestors who founded the group, or even from their parents or grandparents. The Amish do not regard anachronism as a virtue in itself.

At the same time, the Amish tend to be suspicious about inventions, trends, and fads from the outside world. They do not believe that hard work is to be avoided, but regard physical labor as healthy for body and soul. Just because an innovation makes life easier does not mean, from the Amish point of view, that the new way is desirable. Instead, the crucial issue is whether a particular invention or method will help to build community.

By restricting their use of technology, the Amish have been able to maintain a closeness of family and group life that the larger society has lost. The Amish believe that people need

Many of the Amish congregations in Adams County, Indiana, do not permit any use of motors or engines. Animal-powered devices such as these are still common there. These devices may be used for such purposes as pumping water, powering a washing machine, or turning a lathe.

Technology Use in Various Amish Communities

■ Permitted

◪ Permitted in some districts but not others

[*] Natural Gas is permitted

	Pneumatic tools	Bulk milk tank	Mechanical milker	Pickup balers	Tractor for field work	Tractor for belt power	Chain saw	Rototiller	Power lawn mower	Stationary bath tub with running water	Inside flush toilet	Motorized washing machines	Mechanical refrigerator	Propane gas	Pressurized lamps and lanterns
Dover, DE	■					■	■			■	■	■			■
Lancaster, PA	■	■	■	■		■	■		◪	■	■	■	■	■	■
Renno Group, PA	■	◪		■		■	■			■	■	■	◪		■
Nebraska Group, PA				◪			◪					■			
Somerset Co., PA	■	■	■	■	■	■	■	■	■	■	■	■	■		■
Swartzentruber Group, OH	◪											■			
Holmes Co., OH-Andy Weaver	■					■	■			■	■	■		*	■
Holmes Co., OH-Old Order	■			■		■	■	◪	◪	■	■	■	◪	*	■
Holmes Co., OH-New Order	■	■	■	■		■	■	■	■	■	■	■	■	■	■
Geauga Co., OH	■			◪		■	■			■	■	■			■
Adams Co., IN	◪						◪		◪		◪	◪			◪
LaGrange Co., IN	■	◪	◪	◪		■	■	◪	◪	■	■	■	◪	◪	■
Nappanee, IN	■	■	■	■		■	■	■	■	■	■	■	■	■	■
Arthur, IL	■	■	■	■		■	■	■	■	■	■	■	■	■	■
Kalona, IA	■	■	■	■	■	■	■	■	■	■	■	■	■	■	■
Buchanan Co., IA												■			■
Haven, KS	■	■	■	■	■	■	■	■	■	■	■	■	■	■	■
Milverton, ON	■		■				■					■			■
Aylmer, ON	■	■				■	■		■	■	■	■			■
Percentage of all Amish (approximate)	70	35	35	50	6	70	75	20	25	70	70	97	40	30	90

one another more than they need machines, and that many modern conveniences separate people rather than draw them together. A machine that allows one person to do a job that used to require several people may save time, but it prevents a sense of community from developing. The Amish also see folly in a lifestyle that avoids physical labor, then created exercise in the form of jogging or aerobics.

How do the Amish Earn a Living?

In the words of the New Testament, the Amish try not to be "of the world" but cannot avoid being in it. Despite reports to

Harness shops such as this provide for the needs of the Amish community. Machinery is operated with gasoline and diesel engines, air compressors, or hydraulic pumps.

the contrary, the Amish are not self-sufficient. They must take part in the large economic system.

The need to compete with their mechanized neighbors has forced the Amish to weigh the values of human labor and fellowship against economic productivity. Leaders in different communities have chosen to accept differing levels of technology. In some areas, relatively modern items have been accepted in order to keep people on the farm. In other areas, restrictions on agricultural equipment have forced members to seek nonfarm employment, such as factory jobs. Still other communities prohibit modern equipment and at the same time discourage members from working away from home. Leaders in these areas insist that members be satisfied with low-tech farming and home occupations, even if this means a low income.

Each community must decide how much technology can be accepted without disrupting the group's faith and life. This is true of home items as well as farming and business equipment. The most conservative Amish use only the kind of kerosene lamps that appeared around 1850, while the majority of Amish use pressurized gas lamps developed around 1900.

While Amish groups disagree on where to draw the line in regard to innovation, all agree that lines must be drawn. Current popularity is not viewed as an indicator of real need. In fact, worldly approval is seen as a likely sign that an item is not appropriate for a Christian to use. "That which is highly esteemed among men is an abomination unto God," the Amish say, quoting Jesus in the Gospel of Luke. After careful consideration, some innovations have gained acceptance among the Amish, such as windmills, gasoline engines, and batteries. Others have not, including cars, telephones, and electricity.

Amish Ingenuity

The Amish have chosen not to become involved with many areas of modern technology, but they are not averse to inno-

In some Amish communities, ice is still harvested from ponds. It is then used for refrigerating food and cooling milk.

vation within certain technological boundaries. R. P. Schrock, an Amish man from Walnut Creek, Ohio, developed a roller bearing axle for buggies in 1950. Levi Esh of Gordonville, Pennsylvania, made several improvements for gasoline pressure lamps after he began manufacturing them in 1971. Elmo and Mark Stoll of Aylmer, Ontario, designed a greatly improved woodburning cookstove in 1979. In the late 1960s, Martin Schmucker and Melvin Lengacher of Allen County, Indiana, developed a series of horse-powered farming devices, from hay balers to corn pickers.

Other Amish people have tried to manufacture items that are no longer mass produced for the general population. One Amish shop began making kerosene cookstoves after these appliances were no longer available. Many Amish shops manufacture horse-drawn farm machinery.

Some items made for the mainstream are modified to meet Amish requirements. Washing machines are equipped with gasoline engines; electric sewing machines are converted to treadle power; electric refrigerators are converted into ice boxes, and farm machinery meant for tractors is modified for use with horses.

A number of non-electric appliances and tools used by the Amish are still mass produced. Wood- and coal-burning stoves are still in demand among the general population. (Wood stoves are especially popular with "back to basics" people.) Propane refrigerators manufactured for use in recreational vehicles are widely used in Amish kitchens.

The Amish who allow the use of propane and natural gas may use standard gas stoves and water heaters. In addition, many readily-available types of pneumatic shop tools (operated by compressed air) are consistent with Amish requirements.

Some items manufactured primarily for non-industrialized countries also find use among the Amish. Lehman Hardware of Kidron, Ohio, which specializes in non-electric appliances, sells such products as kerosene-operated refrigerators both to the Amish and to foreign missionaries.

Commitment to Ideals

It would be unrealistic to portray the Amish as a society living in unmechanized bliss. Certainly, the Amish way of life would have died long ago if the church's rules did not have strong support from members. As in every religious group, however, some members are not convinced of the ideals of the community. Some Amish men and women are not satisfied with the church's limits on technology and push for change. Some Amish only grudgingly abide by the regulations, and a minority use forbidden items on the sly.

If an Amish group finds it impossible to continue using some form of technology, due to the unavailability of equipment or service, a more modern method is usually adopted. This is true even when it would be possible to go back to an older way.

In one Amish community, for example, ice was delivered by truck to individual homes and used for refrigeration. When the ice company went out of business, the Amish had two options: to use such natural means of refrigeration as flowing water or ice harvested from ponds, or to allow kerosene- or propane-operated appliances, even though Amish groups in many other communities continue to use the older methods.

There are exceptions to the general rule of greater modernization, however. In one Amish community, battery-operated calculators had been accepted for a number of years. Some people became concerned that this was a step toward computerization—a movement seen as a threat to basic Amish ideals. The church decided to reverse the trend and forbade the use of all devices that had a digital display.

One will find among the Amish two basic approaches to technology. The ultra-conservative minority tries for the most part to maintain a pre-electrification way of life typical of rural Americans in the early 1900s. The moderate majority, by contrast, has made concessions to modern technology by adapting many electrical items for use with non-electric sources of energy.

Will the minority be able to continue practicing the old ways? Will the moderate Amish someday adopt all modern technology? Time will tell.

2.
How Do You Light a Room Without Electricity?

ARTHUR, Illinois—Supper was over and the kitchen at the Schrock house was almost pitch dark. Levi Schrock took the lamp from the hook above the table and jiggled it slightly to hear if there was enough fuel in the tank. This lamp burned "white" gasoline or naphtha.

Levi put the lamp on the table and attached a small pump—like one used to inflate bicycle tires—to a valve on the base of the lamp. He vigorously pumped a dozen strokes.

Levi detached the pump and flipped a small wire switch on the upper part of the lamp. This action cleared the gas passageway of dirt. Than he turned a black knob a quarter turn to the left and back again. A small amount of gasoline was forced into a narrow tube, called the generator, by the compressed air inside the tank.

Levi quickly lit two large wooden matches at the same time and held the flames to the generator. Their combined heat vaporized the liquid gasoline. After a few seconds two small white bags—called mantles—began to flame. An adjustment to the knob extinguished the flames, and the mantles began to radiate with intense light. The lamp gave a slight hissing sound.

Levi turned the knob all the way on. He hung the lamp back on a hook in the middle of a round metal deflector, which protected the ceiling from the heat of the lamp.

Lizzie Schrock and her daughters began clearing the table of dishes and taking them to the sink. Levi put on his coat and hat and grabbed a lantern from a shelf on the porch. This lantern was much the same as the lamp, except that it had only one mantle. The lantern was enclosed in a glass globe and had a metal top with a carrying ring.

Levi pumped the self-contained pump on the lantern and lit it in the same way as the lamp. Twelve-year-old Joe followed his father to the barn.

An additional lamp was lit at the sink while the women washed the dishes. Then Lizzie went to the enclosed porch to her sewing machine. Here she lit another lamp. This one had two mantles at the end of a long pipe extending from the middle of a small propane tank enclosed in a wooden cabinet. The tank was like those used for a gas grill. The lamp was on casters so that it could be rolled from place to place.

The girls and their two youngest brothers occupied themselves under the kitchen light with games and projects. Levi and Joe returned after doing the chores and joined the rest of the family.

The clock struck nine, signalling the time for the family to settle down for the night. After the evening prayer the two oldest children, Joe and Rachel, took flashlights and led their brothers and sisters upstairs to the bedrooms.

Rachel entered the girls' room and directed the beam of the flashlight to a lamp on a table beside the bed. She took the glass chimney from the lamp and got a wooden match from a small container. After striking the match she held the flame to the bit of kerosene-soaked wick protruding above the brass fixture. This lamp was not nearly so bright as the pressurized mantle lamp, and its light was yellowish.

Rachel put the chimney back on the lamp and adjusted the wick with a small knob so that the flame was neither too low nor too high. If the flame were too high, it would smoke.

The younger girls snuggled into bed in the unheated room, but Rachel spent a few minutes reading and writing before blowing out the light.

3.
Lanterns and Lamps

In Amish homes light does not appear at the flick of a switch. Considerable care must be taken to light non-electric lamps and to keep them in working condition.

Lighting devices vary somewhat from group to group. The most conservative Amish use only the old flat-wick kerosene lamps. The majority of Amish make limited use of this kind of lamp, but get most of their light from other sources. Few if any Amish have used candles as a primary lighting source since the end of the 19th century.

Kerosene Lamps

Kerosene, or "coal oil," lamps first appeared in the larger society in the 1850s. They gained popularity with the development of the petroleum industry, soon replacing lamps fueled by whale oil, burning fluid (turpentine and alcohol), and lard oil.

A great variety of kerosene lamps soon developed. A popular improvement on the flat-wick version was the round-wick, central draft model, known as the Rochester lamp. Patented in 1884, this lamp could produce light equivalent to a 40-watt electric bulb, compared to the 10-watt equivalent of a regular kerosene lamp.

Many Amish use the old-style kerosene lanterns which were popular for many years among farmers. Lanterns of this type have been manufactured by the R. E. Dietz Company of Syracuse, New York, since 1867. Similar lanterns with red

The most common type of lamp used in Amish homes burns naphtha or "white" gasoline, which is forced to the incandescent mantles by compressed air.

lenses are used as buggy lights by the most conservative Amish groups.

Pressure Lamps

The majority of Old Order Amish use lamps that burn "white," or clear, gasoline or naphtha. The fuel tank in these lamps is filled with compressed air. The air forces the fuel to the generator tube, where it is vaporized, and then to the mantles, where it is burned.

Mantles are loosely woven fabric bags treated with a rare earth mineral called thorium. Before actual use, the fiber of the mantles is burned away, leaving only a fragile mineral skeleton. When the lamp is lit, the mantles glow very brightly but do not flame after the first few seconds.

History of Gas and Gasoline Lamps

The portable gas lamps used by the Amish adapt technology from the stationary gas systems of the 18th and 19th centuries. Artificially-produced gas was first used in England at the end of the 1700s. The first municipal gas plant in the United States was established in Baltimore in 1817.

By the time of the Civil War, nearly 300 urban areas had gas service. Initially, this gas was used to light streets, factories, and large public buildings, but eventually it found its way into private homes.

People without access to city gas could make their own by using the "gas machines" that became available in the 1860s. These produced gas from gasoline and piped the fuel to lighting fixtures throughout the house. Systems that burned carbide or acetylene developed later. Beginning in the 1890s, "hollow wire" systems used brass tubes to distribute pressurized liquid gasoline from a central source.

Incandescent mantles were invented in 1885 by Karl Auer Van Welsbach of Austria. Used with piped-in gas, they produced brighter artificial light than anything known before. Gas mantle lights were even brighter than the original incandescent electric bulb, invented by Thomas Edison in 1879.

Self-contained gasoline pressure lamps came on the scene just before the turn of the century. For the first time a source of intense light was truly portable. Even so, the new pressure lamps did not become popular for home use until William C. Coleman developed a portable reading lamp in 1908. The Coleman Company, which he founded, produced pressurized mantle lamps in the United States until 1951 and in Canada until 1973.

In 1965 an Amish man from Lancaster County, Pennsylvania—Levi Esh—started a business to provide parts and repairs for lamps of this type. In 1971, with the sanction of the Coleman company, Esh began the Leacock Lamp Manufacturing Company. Using the Coleman system, Esh pro-

The most conservative Amish groups use only old-style kerosene lamps. These are used as an auxiliary source of light in most Amish homes.

duces lamps for the continuing Amish market. These lamps burn white (clear) gas, Coleman fuel (naphtha) or kerosene.

Pressurized mantle lanterns for outdoor use have been available from the Coleman Company since 1914 and remain popular with campers. Many Amish people use these lanterns outside the house, and sometimes inside in place of regular table lamps.

Pressurized mantle lamps can produce the equivalent of a 100-watt electric bulb, and some people actually consider them too bright. An alternative is the Aladdin lamp, which combines a round wick, like a Rochester lamp, with an incandescent mantle.

First introduced in 1909, Aladdins are not pressurized and produce light equal to a 60-watt bulb. Aladdin lamps are still being made and find occasional use among the Amish.

Centralized Lighting Systems

In a few Amish communities, stationary wall or ceiling lights are fueled by pipelines from a central propane tank. Many of the "New Order" Amish in Ohio have this kind of lighting system in their homes. In Indiana, Illinois, and elsewhere, this type of centralized system is used by Amish shops and businesses.

Pressurized kerosene or gasoline systems are nearly identical to the old hollow wire systems and require the tank to be periodically filled with compressed air.

In a few Holmes County shops, natural gas provides light. Centralized natural gas systems use fuel obtained from a well. In individual houses, gas is often used for heating, cooking, and refrigeration.

In Lancaster County, large chicken-raising businesses have a unique method of lighting. Individual pressure lanterns are attached to a centralized compressed air system. The lamps

Non-electric pole lamps, at left, have become common since the 1960s. On the right, a gasoline lantern hangs suspended from a disconnected electric fixture.

The Amish try to use natural lighting from windows as much as possible for activities during daylight hours. These are "Nebraska," or "White-Top," Amish women from central Pennsylvania.

are lit in the usual way and hung in the chicken house. Air lines, but not fuel lines, are attached to valves on the lanterns. A battery-operated timer shuts off the air at a given time, thus extinguishing the lanterns.

Other Kinds of Lights

Long-stemmed floor lamps that have individual propane tanks are becoming increasingly popular in many Amish communities. The tank is portable and often enclosed in a wooden cabinet on casters.

Other floor lamps use pressurized gasoline or kerosene. The tanks for these lights need to be filled with compressed air from a pump, like regular Coleman and Leacock lamps and lanterns.

Flashlights operated by dry cell batteries are used by nearly all Amish. In addition, most Amish use battery-operated lights and flashers on their buggies. In some cases the batteries for these lights are recharged on the generators used to operate dairy equipment. In communities where generators are not allowed, batteries are taken to a non-Amish business for recharging.

Ben Fisher, a Lancaster County Amish man, developed a battery especially suited for Amish vehicle lights. Fisher began the Pequea Battery Company in Ronks, Pennsylvania, in the late 1950s to manufacture these heavy-duty storage units.

4.
How Do You Cook With a Wood Stove?

BERNE, Indiana—The mantel clock was striking five o'clock as Katie Schwartz sleepily made her way from the bedroom to the kitchen. She went to the black kitchen stove and pulled out the air intake level on its side. After pausing a moment to avoid getting a cloud of smoke in her face, she grasped the detachable handle protruding from the stove top and lifted the circular lid over the fire box. She was delighted to see an abundance of glowing embers. Since she had gotten this new airtight stove, she no longer had to start a fire every morning.

Katie stirred the coals with an iron poker, then laid several sticks of wood on top of them. She replaced the lid on top of the stove and adjusted the damper controls on the side so that more air would pass over the fire. Katie was glad that the ashes did not need to be cleaned out of the stove often. Doing so used to be one of her regular chores.

Filling a teapot with water from the hand pump, Katie set the container at the front of the stove. This, she knew, was the hottest part of the top. There was no quick, easy way to control the heat on a wood-burning stove. A measure of control was gained by shifting pans from place to place and by changing the draft on the fire.

Katie peeked into the fire box to observe flames rolling from the wood. She closed the lid and adjusted the dampers so that less air would fan the flames. A roaring fire was not best for most cooking.

As Abe and the two boys came in from the barn, Katie placed a greased, cast iron skillet on top of the stove. She cracked a half dozen eggs in the large sizzling pan. When the eggs were sufficiently fried, she put them on a plate and placed them in the oven so they would keep warm.

Seven-year-old Susie set the table while Katie was cooking. When Abe and the four children were seated at the table, Katie took her place. The Schwartzes bowed their heads for a silent prayer. After grace was said, Katie put the eggs on the table and began frying more.

Abe and the children helped themselves to thick slices of bread, which they spread with butter and strawberry jam. All the family members kept a small piece of bread with which to thoroughly clean the egg from their plates.

The meal also included milk and homemade granola. Ten-year-old Levi had the job of bringing in milk from the milk house every morning. The Schwartzes had no refrigerator.

After the breakfast dishes were washed, Katie began her weekly task of making bread. As she did every Friday, she combined warm water, lard, salt, sugar, and yeast in a bowl. After letting the mixture stand, she stirred in several cups of flour and beat the combination until it was smooth.

Katie added more flour and vigorously kneaded the resulting dough with greased hands for about 15 minutes. Susie watched the process with keen interest. She was allowed to put her hands in the dough briefly, before Katie set it aside to rise. The dough was placed some distance from the stove, so that the warmth did not speed the action of the yeast and produce crumbly bread.

While Katie waited for the dough, she began slicing carrots, onions, and potatoes for a stew and putting them in a large pot. In the cellar, she chose a jar of green beans and a jar of home-canned beef from the ample shelves. Since the Schwartzes had no freezer, they canned most of their food, including meat.

When an hour and a half had passed, Katie took the enlarged dough and punched it down gently with her fists. Then she returned it to its place for another hour of rising. With Susie's help, she mixed the stew in a large stainless steel pot and put it at the back of the stove. Here it would simmer until lunch time.

The dough was punched down once more before it was divided and shaped into loaf-sized portions. Then it was placed into metal pans and allowed to rise another hour.

Katie added more wood to the fire box and adjusted the dampers to the positions she had learned would create the proper temperature. She watched the thermometer on the front of the oven until it stabilized at 350 degrees.

Six pans of dough were placed in the oven—two

more than would fit in Katie's old stove. Katie and Susie peeked in the oven periodically to check the progress of the baking. After half an hour, the golden brown loaves were removed.

The tantalizing aroma of stew and freshly baked bread greeted Abe as he came in from the barn.

5.
The Amish Kitchen

Three main types of cookstoves are used by the Amish. The most conservative groups and others who have easy access to wood still favor wood-burning stoves. Kerosene stoves, usually called oil stoves, also are widely used, while propane (bottled gas) stoves have been accepted in a number of Amish communities.

Wood-Burning Cookstoves

No group of Amish currently makes use of open fireplaces for cooking. A few "Nebraska," or "White-Top," Amish of central Pennsylvania (so named for their founder's place of origin and the color of their buggies) use old-fashioned bake ovens. These are especially popular when large amounts of baked goods are needed for church services or weddings. Bake ovens are made of brick or stone and are usually located in separate small buildings.

These ovens were typical of other Pennsylvania Germans until the early part of this century. The Amish in Lancaster County, Pennsylvania, used bake ovens as late as the 1930s.

Iron cookstoves were very rare in the general society before the 1830s or 40s. Before this time almost all cooking was done in open fireplaces. Iron heating stoves had developed before the 19th century, but these were rarely used for food preparation.

The change from fireplaces to cookstoves took place very gradually, but was nearly complete by 1880. The Amish seem to have followed the general trend.

Wood-burning cookstoves (left) are still common in many Amish communities. Kettle stoves (right) are used for many purposes including heating water for washing clothes. Here, apple butter is being made in a very large kettle.

Several North American and European companies still make wood-burning cookstoves. A number of types are used by the Amish.

In the 1970s two Amish brothers from Aylmer, Ontario, Elmo and Mark Stoll, decided to design a cookstove that was more fuel efficient and easier to use than available models. The two men wanted to utilize the downdraft system that was typical of heating stoves but not found in any cookstoves. They thought a stove should be airtight so that heat would not escape up the flue unnecessarily, and that a larger oven should be provided. In addition, the brothers wished for a firebox that would hold enough wood to burn through the night.

Elmo and Mark studied the pros and cons of available cookstoves and incorporated the best features into a design of their own. The result was the Pioneer Maid stove, which first appeared in 1979. These plain, black stoves are manufactured at an Amish shop in Aylmer and are very popular in many Amish communities.

In some areas where wood is not plentiful, coal-burning cookstoves are used. These work basically the same as a wood stove but have a firebrick lining which is capable of handling the more intense heat of coal.

Kerosene-Burning Stoves

Kerosene and gasoline stoves became available in the 1860s, following the development of the petroleum industry. Kerosene-burning stoves are popular in many Amish communities. Some families use them for all their cooking, others in addition to a wood-burning stove. Many people prefer to use a kerosene stove in the summer and a wood stove in the winter.

"Oil" stoves (which burn kerosene) are used in addition to wood stoves by some Amish. Others use them as the sole cooking range.

Propane gas is used for cooking, refrigeration, space heating, and heating water in several large Amish communities.

This is because of the greater heat generated by a wood stove. Often the kerosene stove is located in the "summer kitchen," which may be in a basement or semi-attached room.

The Amish prefer the Perfection brand of kerosene wick-type stove. These were made in Cleveland, Ohio, until about 1960. Because of decreased demand in the United States, the manufacture of these stoves was shifted to the South American nation of Colombia. The Amish purchased some of these South American-made stoves until production there was discontinued about 10 years later.

Rebuilt Perfection stoves and stove parts remain available from Lehman's Hardware of Kidron, Ohio, and several Amish-owned businesses. In addition, the D. L. Schwartz Company of northern Indiana makes kerosene stoves of a similar design exclusively for the Amish market.

Cooking with Gas

In several large Amish communities, bottled gas is allowed. In Lancaster County, the Amish have been using this fuel since the 1950s. Amish who are permitted to use bottled gas cook on gas ranges like those used by non-Amish people.

The current variety of bottled gas, also known as propane or liquefied petroleum gas (LP), was developed in 1912 but did not become widely available until the 1930s. An earlier and much more expensive type of bottled gas, called Blaugas, had been used by wealthy rural people since the early 1900s.

In areas such as Ohio, Kansas, and Illinois, natural gas is sometimes used. Some groups view the presence of gas deposits on an Amish farm as providential, while others see it

Coleman camp stoves are preferred in summer in many Amish kitchens, when the extra heat from a wood stove is not needed.

If a farm is blessed with a spring, the cold, flowing water may be used to keep food cool.

as a temptation. In certain Amish groups, only members who have a well on their own land are permitted to use natural gas. In the most conservative groups it may not be used at all, regardless of its source.

In LaGrange County, Indiana, and Holmes County, Ohio, some Amish use gas stoves converted to a gasoline pressure system. These stoves operate on the same principle as models that were built in the 1930s, as well as small Coleman camp stoves that are still being manufactured. In many Amish communities, the Coleman models find wide use as auxiliary stoves.

Refrigeration

The most conservative Amish groups use only natural refrigeration for food items. In cold weather, setting perishables outside or in unheated parts of the house suffices. In warm weather, cellars and wells provide a limited cooling effect. The underground temperature stays at the annual above-ground average. This varies somewhat according to region; in eastern Pennsylvania it is about 54 degrees Fahrenheit.

If a farm in fortunate enough to have a spring on it premises, the natural chill of the flowing water is used to preserve food. A small stone or brick building is built over the spring, or the house is constructed so that the spring is in the basement. The water is routed through cement compartments and channels where food containers are placed.

Water pumped from wells or cisterns is used for cooling in much the same way. Sometimes food is simply placed in buckets of water to cool.

Ice Refrigeration

Ice is used for refrigeration in a number of Amish communities. Some Amish in northern areas, such as Iowa,

This modern-looking refrigerator in Geauga County, Ohio, has been stripped of its electrical apparatus and converted to an ice box. Old-style ice boxes and ice chests are still found in some of the most conservative Amish communities.

Wisconsin, and Ontario, still obtain ice from ponds and lakes. Ice harvesting is a community effort in which many men gather to cut out large blocks with special motorized saws and hand saws. Ice is stored in specially-insulated ice houses.

The use of ice for refrigeration did not become popular in North America until the 1830s. About this time an invention appeared that made it possible to cut ice into neat blocks by means of a horse-drawn device. The use of ice increased very rapidly through the rest of the century.

Between 1860 and 1910, natural ice was gradually replaced by manufactured ice. But ice refrigeration remained widespread until the end of World War II. Nearly one-third of all U.S. households still used ice boxes in 1944, despite the availability of electricity and mechanical refrigeration.

Ice Delivery

Although the ice man was a familiar figure for the first half of the 20th century, the occupation became nearly extinct in the 1950s. But rural ice delivery survives in several Amish communities. There is an active ice route in Geauga County, Ohio, where the Amish use ice boxes as the primary means of refrigeration. Ice delivery also remains available to the minority of Amish in Holmes County who still use ice refrigeration, and to members of several smaller communities.

In some areas the Amish must pick up their own ice from vendors. This is the case in Adams County, Indiana.

Many of the Amish who use ice for refrigeration still have the old-style ice boxes and ice chests. Now that these are no longer manufactured, some Amish have resorted to converting electric refrigerators to ice boxes. The ice blocks are placed in the redesigned freezer compartment.

Non-Electric Mechanical Refrigerators

A large percentage of Amish districts permit non-electric mechanical refrigerators. These operate on the absorption sys-

This gasoline-powered saw is used to cut ice blocks from ponds in Buchanan County, Iowa.

tem by which a kerosene or propane flame cools a compartment through evaporation and condensation.

Such refrigerators appeared first in Sweden in 1922 and were being made in the United States by 1925. The largest manufacturer was the Servel Company, which produced gas refrigerators from 1926 to 1956.

The Swedish-based Domestic Company and the Swiss-based Sibir Company have U.S. plants that still produce absorption refrigerators. Both firms sell both propane and kerosene models.

In North America, gas refrigerators are made primarily for use in recreational vehicles and hotel rooms. Some Amish people are displeased with the small size of these appliances.

In Mifflin and Somerset counties in Pennsylvania, some Amish families connect refrigeration coils from their milk cooling systems to home refrigerators and coolers. In Lancaster County, food coolers refrigerated in this way are used as an auxiliary to gas refrigerators.

A gas refrigerator and range are found in this Lancaster Amish kitchen. The wood stove is used only in cold weather.

Frozen Food Lockers

Even in a full-sized gas or kerosene refrigerator, the freezing compartment offers little space to store frozen food. A few Amish keep such items in a gas or kerosene freezer. Others rent space in the frozen food lockers operated in some small towns and rural areas, often by grocery stores.

Lockers of this sort used to be quite common, but now are rare except in Amish areas. The practice of renting out space in large, commercially-owned freezers began in the 1930s and was quite popular until the 1950s, when home freezers made this service largely unnecessary.

Most Amish people neither own freezers nor rent locker space. Instead, they simply do without frozen foods, as all people did in the not-so-distant past.

These Amish rely on home-canned food. Their pantries and cellars are filled with hundreds of glass jars containing many kinds of fruit and vegetables. Even meat, such as beef, chicken, and sausage, are stored in this way.

Other Kitchen Appliances

Most of the smaller appliances found in modern kitchens are noticeably absent among the Amish. Electric-powered items, such as toasters, toaster ovens, mixers, blenders, coffee makers, food processors, electric knives, electric can openers, electric frying pans, crock pots, dishwashers, garbage disposals, and microwave ovens, cannot be used by Amish people. The Amish simply use tools and methods common in the pre-electric era.

The Lancaster County Amish have found that some kitchen tools can be converted to run on compressed air, rather than electricity. (Shop tools can also be powered this way. See Chapters 24 and 25). Air-operated "kitchen centers" are especially popular. These appliances can be used as mixers, blenders, food grinders, slicers, shredders, salad-makers, or dough-makers.

6.
How Do You Get Hot Water Without an Electric Pump or Heater?

APPLE CREEK, Ohio—Abe Hershberger walked through the April evening to the steel windmill tower on a hill above the house. He engaged the mechanism that started the pump into motion. There was a good breeze today, he noted, more than enough to pump the water.

Water was soon running through a pipe from the well into a tank beneath the enclosed front porch of the house. When this reservoir overflowed, the excess was directed to a tank beneath the wash house, and from there to the milk house.

The lay of the land on Abe's farm enabled him to use gravity flow. Few Amish farmers were so fortunate, even in this rolling section of eastern Ohio.

The water in the milk house flowed into a long cement trough. Here the milk cans would be placed for cooling. From the milk house, the water flowed to the watering trough for the livestock and then into the farm pond. The water in the farm system was replaced with fresh water twice a day, and went first to the house before circulating to the other buildings.

In the kitchen Abe's wife, Leah, and 12-year-old daughter, Miriam, cleared the last of the supper dishes and stacked them on one end of the dry sink. Leah took a steaming tea kettle from the cookstove and poured its contents into the dishpans in the metal-lined sink. Miriam brought a bucket of cold water from a pump in the kitchen. This was the only way to get water from the tank.

Miriam mingled the cold water with hot in the dishpans until it was just the right temperature. She and her mother quickly washed the dishes for the family of six.

When the dishes were all dried and put away, Leah and Miriam tended to a weekly ritual—the Saturday night bath. From now through summer, they would use the wash house in the backyard for bathing. In colder weather the bathtub was placed beside the kitchen stove.

Miriam gathered pieces of wood from the shed beside the wash house, while Leah filled a bucket with water from the hand pump inside the building. The water was poured into a large iron kettle encased in brick. This kettle was not only used to heat bath water, but to heat water for washing clothes. When it was the Hershbergers' turn to have church at their farm, the kettle was used to make the traditional bean soup for the noon meal.

Miriam opened an iron door beneath the kettle and inserted the wood. She lit a fire, then went to the house with her mother.

An hour later, after the water had a chance to heat, Miriam came back to the wash house. She took down the large galvanized bathtub from the wall, dipped out steaming water from the kettle, and poured it into the tub. She added enough cold water from the pump to make the temperature comfortable.

Leah returned from the house with her two youngest children—Lizzie, five, and Mary, two. The two girls were put in the tub at the same time. When their bath was finished, the tub was emptied and refilled for seven-year-old Mose, who was beckoned from the barn. Miriam and her 10-year-old brother, Levi, filled their own tubs.

Abe enjoyed his bath after he finished milking. At last, as the sun set, Leah stepped into the tub for a few minutes' soaking. The Psalms spoke of a clean heart, she reflected, but it was also good to be clean on the outside, especially before tomorrow's church service.

7.
Amish Plumbing

The Amish use a wide range of methods to pump, heat, and circulate water. The extent to which modern plumbing is used depends on how conservative a particular group or community is.

Old-fashioned hand pumps are still common among the more traditional Amish. These pumps may be inside or outside the house. A small "pitcher" pump is often found in the kitchen, mounted on a simple sink.

Members of the most conservative groups have no pump at

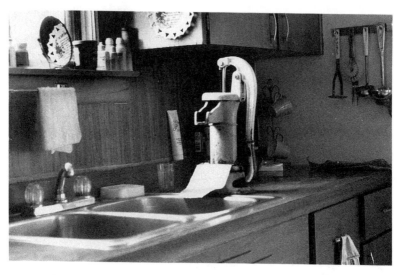

In an Ohio Amish kitchen, an old-fashioned pitcher pump provides cistern water for washing, and a modern tap brings drinking water from the well.

This Ohio Amish girl must work to quench her thirst.

the sink where dishes are washed. Instead, water is carried to an old-style dry sink—a low cabinet with a recessed top that is lined with metal or another waterproof material. Dishes are washed in dishpans on top of the sink. Water must also be carried away from the dry sink; there is no drain.

If a farm is blessed with a spring on its property, flowing water is piped into the house or the house is built over the water source. In Mifflin County, Pennsylvania, water is piped down from mountain streams.

In addition to using surface and underground water, many Amish collect rainwater from their house roofs. This is usually stored in a cistern and is not used for drinking water. A pitcher pump usually serves to draw cistern water.

Windmills

Windmill towers topped by large, flower-like fans are a common sight in most Amish communities. Windmills are often used to pump water into elevated storage tanks and to fill water reservoirs near or under the house which are tapped by hand "pitcher" pumps.

Water storage tanks may be situated in barns, in the attics of houses, or on a higher elevation of land. Large railroad tank cars (minus their undercarriage and wheels) are sometimes turned on end for use as water tanks. From these holding vessels, water flows by gravity through pipes to spigots at the house and barn.

Windmill History

The American-style windmill mounted on a tower was introduced in 1854 by Daniel Halladay of Vermont. Unlike Dutch and other European windmills, these windmills adjusted automatically to the direction of the wind.

During the oil crisis of the 1970s, there was a revival of interest in windmills and a wide variety of models were put on the market. Many of these were meant for generating electricity, however, and so found little use among the Amish.

The windmill here pumps water into a storage tank. The water flows by gravity to the house and barn, making possible modern plumbing without a pressurized system.

Several companies still make traditional water-pumping windmills. The oldest are Aermotor, now of San Angelo, Texas; Heller-Aller of Napoleon, Ohio; Dempster of Beatrice, Nebraska; and Verdun of Hutchinson, Kansas. Aermotor windmills were made in Argentina from 1969 to 1982, and the Fiasa company in that country still manufactures windmills of the Aermotor type.

In addition to new windmills, renovated models are popular among the Amish. In some communities, Amish people have made a business of buying old windmills and repairing them.

The "Nebraska," or "White-Top," Amish of central Pennsylvania are alone among the Old Order groups in prohibiting windmills. In the more progressive Amish communities, however, windmills are used much less than in earlier times.

Water Wheels

In Lancaster County, Pennsylvania, a unique system of pumping water has been used for many years. Small water wheels encased in concrete housings are placed in streams. The turning of the wheel by the flow of water is translated into a back and forth motion on a heavy wire leading to a water pump.

Sometimes the distance from the water wheel to the pump is quite great, necessitating the use of supporting poles for the wire. The poles and wires often resemble electrical wires. Thus, the system is called "Amish electricity."

In the early 1980s, Amishman Ben King of Lancaster County, Pennsylvania, devised an improved water wheel. King's model featured a paddy wheel rather than the traditional overshot wheel. A power takeoff assembly, like that used on tractors, was utilized instead of a crankshaft. The new design worked more smoothly and efficiently than old-style pumping wheels. Its development, however, did not halt a steady decline in the use of water wheels.

Another old but increasingly rare method of pumping water among the Amish is the hydraulic ram. Water from a stream is piped into the ram device which, by means of water pressure

Water wheels that pump well water are increasingly being replaced by pneumatic pumps on Amish farms in Lancaster County, Pennsylvania.

and air pressure, pumps the water to a storage tank. No other power source is needed. The ram works best when there is a steep decline between the water source and the mechanism.

Engines to Pump Water

Except for Adams County, Indiana, where most church districts use windmills and hand pumps exclusively, nearly every Amish community permits the use of gas or diesel engines to pump water. Engines are even allowed among such conservative groups as the Nebraska Amish and Swartzentruber Amish.

In some communities, all the water is pumped by engines. In others, engines provide power when other methods cannot be used, such as when there is too little wind to run a windmill.

Pressurized water systems are used in many of the larger Amish communities. Air that has been compressed by gas or diesel engines forces water through the system.

Submersible well pumps that run on compressed air are popular in some Amish settlements. Pumps of this type were originally produced by Westinghouse, beginning in 1919. In 1965, long after manufacturing of these pumps had ceased, an Old Order Mennonite named Daniel Stauffer began making similar pumps in his small shop near Ephrata, Pennsylvania. More recently, another Old Order Mennonite in the same area—Ervin Hoover—started to manufacture submersible pneumatic pumps.

Modern Kitchens and Bathrooms

Amish that have pressurized or even gravity-flow water systems can have modern plumbing without electric pumps. More than half of all Amish houses are so equipped.

Amish kitchens and bathrooms in such large settlements as Lancaster County; Nappanee, Indiana; and Arthur, Illinois; look and function almost the same as those of non-Amish people. The majority of Amish in Holmes and Geauga counties in

Even in Amish communities where modern bathrooms are permitted in homes, outhouses are still typical for schools.

Wood-burning water heaters such as this one are manufactured in Amish shops. The Amish also use gas and kerosene water heaters.

Ohio and LaGrange County, Indiana, also have modern plumbing, including indoor bathrooms with flush toilets and built-in bathtubs and showers.

Old-fashioned outhouses are still used by the most conservative Amish groups. In many communities that allow modern plumbing in homes, only hand pumps and outhouses are used at Amish schools.

Heating Water

Water heaters further modernize many Amish homes. In some communities, bottled gas is used to heat water. Among some of the more conservative groups, however, only wood, coal, or kerosene water heaters are permitted.

Some Amish shops have started making wood and coal water heaters. New kerosene heaters are no longer available, but used models are eagerly sought. In Holmes County, members of groups that have recently permitted gas water heaters sell their old kerosene heaters to members who are not permitted to use gas.

A few Amish, such as the Renno group of Mifflin County, Pennsylvania, heat water by piping it through a "water front" or "water jacket" device attached to a wood-burning stove. This method became popular in the larger society in the early 1900s.

In the most conservative groups, no water heaters of any kind are used. Large quantities of water are heated in kettles built into brick stoves in the wash house or on small cast iron laundry stoves. Water for many domestic uses is heated in tea kettles on these stoves or in tanks called "reservoirs" attached to the sides of a cookstove.

8.

How Do You Keep Warm Without Centralized Heating?

LA GRANGE, Indiana—Jake Borntrager poked his head out from beneath the warm covers, hesitant to face the cold morning. Then, with a surge of energy, he burst from his cocoon and went to the window.

His sleepy eyes squinted as he beheld the brilliant blanket of white, radiant even at this hour. He smiled, for he knew the snow would make one of the day's jobs easier—hauling wood.

Jake dressed quickly, then refueled the fire in the heater. He opened the door of the brown metallic box in the dining area and saw the glow of a few burning coals. He raked the coals together with a small hoe-like tool and inserted several small pieces of wood on top of them. Finally, he added split logs and shut the door. From experience he knew the heat of the coals would be sufficient to ignite the wood.

Dan and Andy, the teenage twins, were soon downstairs and went with Jake to do the morning milking. After a hearty breakfast, the trio went to the implement shed and extricated the bobsled from the tangle of tools. They hitched a team of

Belgian horses to the sled and enjoyed a smooth ride over the fields to the wood lot.

Jake guided the sled close to a white oak tree about one and a half feet in diameter. Ordinarily white oak would not be used for fire wood, but this tree was partly hollow and scrubby. It would be of little value for lumber.

Jake carefully managed the trees on his four-acre wood lot, harvesting them selectively. In this way a continuous supply of wood was ensured.

With a careful eye, Jake studied the oak to determine which way the tree leaned and whether the branches were heavier on one side than the other. It was important to know which direction the tree would fall, so that everyone could get out of the way.

Jake took a chain saw from the sled and cranked it to a roaring start. He began by cutting a large notch near the base of the tree. When this was finished he made a deep, angled cut in the opposite side of the trunk. When he reached the desired depth, Jake jerked the blade from the trunk and stepped back several paces. The tree groaned and crackled as it began toppling, then wooshed to a crash on the forest floor.

Jake began cutting off the branches, which the two boys dragged away. Most of these would also be cut up; very little wood was wasted.

The trunk Jake cut into 18-inch lengths, just right for the stoves. Dan and Andy were kept busy stacking the wood on the sled. The temperature was only about 20 degrees Fahrenheit, but the constant activity kept each of the Borntragers quite warm. "Wood heats twice," Jake though to himself, remembering the old saying, "once when you cut it and once when you burn it."

Still, the job was much easier than it had been in his youth, he reflected. Then, no power cutting tools were used, only axes and two-man crosscut saws. Some of Abe's cousins in other Amish communities still did it that way.

The chain saw made quick work of the tree, and by noon the oak was completely sectioned and on the sled. The Borntragers took the load back to the farmstead and stacked the pieces in the open-sided woodshed. They would gather more wood later in the day.

Today's cutting would not provide heat until next fall or winter. Freshly-cut wood has a high moisture content and does not burn well, so this load would be allowed to dry for anywhere from six months to a year. To speed up the process, the sections needed to be split further. This job would provide hours of ax work for Dan and Andy. Little brother Ben's responsibility was to keep the wood box filled in the house.

In the evening the Borntrager family gathered around the heater and cookstove in the kitchen and living room. The oven door was left open to circulate more heat. This also was a favorite place to perch cold, wet feet. Wet gloves and boots were hung from the drying rack above the stove.

Registers in the ceiling allowed some warmth to rise into the upstairs bedrooms, but in winter that part of the house seldom reached a comfortable temperature for sitting. The children were not tempted to go off by themselves, away from the heater.

9.
The Home Fires

One might assume, considering their non-electric ways, that the Amish still heat their houses by the traditional open-hearth method. However, while they have not adopted modern centralized heating, neither have they preserved the heating system typical of pioneer log cabins.

The Amish typically heat their homes with one or more heating stoves on the first floor of the house. In some homes a cookstove serves as a supplementary heater or the sole source of heat. Kerosene heaters also are widely used as an auxiliary source of warmth.

Most heating stoves burn wood or coal, although a sizeable minority of Amish (more than one-third) use propane or natural gas heaters. Communities that use gas for cooking do not necessarily use it for heating. In Lancaster County, for example, propane is typically used for cooking, but coal, wood, and kerosene are the usual fuels for heating.

Unlike some items needed for the Amish lifestyle, appropriate heating devices are readily available. In such area as Berne, Indiana, and Ashland, Ohio, Amish shops manufacture nonelectric heaters. In addition, many non-Amish companies produce wood-burning stoves for ecologically inclined consumers.

The wood and coal heaters chosen by the Amish are rather plain, squarish, and very functional. A model of coal heater popular among the Amish features an automatic thermostat. This stove can operate up to 48 hours on one filling of coal and

Three types of space heaters are shown here: a coal heater from Lancaster County, Pennsylvania (upper left); wood heater from Geauga County, Ohio (upper right); and propane gas heater from Kalona, Iowa (bottom).

Wood is burned for cooking and heating in many Amish communities. Hauling heavy loads on sleds rather than wagons reduces strain on the horses.

heat up to five rooms. Some wood heaters have similar features.

In Ohio some Amish place wood or coal heaters in their basements and put a metal jacket over the stove with ducts extending to registers in several rooms on the first floor. Unlike centralized heating systems, however, there is no blower to force the hot air, and there are no ducts reaching to the second floor.

Wood Stove History

Although heating stoves were relatively rare in North America until the mid-1800s, the Pennsylvania Germans (pre-

Legend for Chart on Right

	Period of increasing or declining use
■■■	Period of common use
——	Continuing use among Amish
O	Used by few if any Amish
C	Used by the more conservative Amish
L	Used by the more liberal Amish
M	Used by the majority of the Amish
E	Used by the small minority of Amish who allow electricity

[1]Used as an alternate light source in most Amish homes.
[2]Rules on phone use vary widely. Only a few Amish have phones in their homes.
[3]No Old Order Amish permit members to own or drive cars, but riding in cars is usually allowed.

Technological History in America Compared to Current Amish Technology

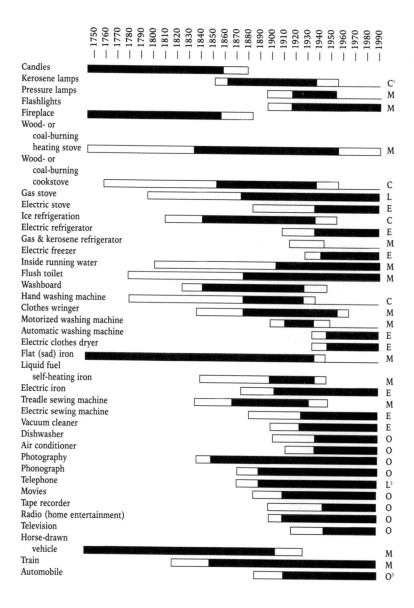

sumably including the Amish) appear to have used them from the time of their arrival in the New World. This was long before Benjamin Franklin's famous stove of 1742.

A very simple, but effective, cast iron box called a five-plate or jamb stove was used by German settlers as early as the first quarter of the 18th century. The earliest stoves were merely projections from the back of the centrally located fireplace, but they provided more-even heating than fireplaces located at one end of the house. There is evidence that Mennonite settler Christian Herr used such a stove in his house (popularly identified with his father, Hans), which was built in 1719 near Lancaster, Pennsylvania.

Another type of stove found in colonial Pennsylvania was the six-plate stove. This stove had its own flue and was independent of the fireplace. The six-plate design developed into the ten-plate stove, which featured a small oven. Both types were used in Holland as early as the 17th century but were not introduced to Pennsylvania until the 1760s. These stoves were the prototypes of later cooking and heating stoves, which did not catch on among non-Germanic Americans until the 1840s.

Centralized heating systems did not become popular until the 20th century. As late as 1940 only one-third of all American households had central heating.

10.

How Can You Wash Clothes Without an Electric Washer and Dryer?

MOUNT HOPE, Ohio—Barbara Yoder and her teenage daughter, Irene, finished sorting the Monday morning laundry. Irene filled the washing machine with buckets of hot water tapped from the wood-burning water heater. After adding soap powder to the water, she put a load of sheets and pillow cases into the washing machine. Barbara filled two washtubs, one with warm water and a little bleach and the other with cooler water and some fabric softener. Cold water was carried from the hand pump outside.

Irene gave a yank on the starting cord, sending the gasoline engine beneath the washer humming. She turned the knob on the other side of the machine, which started the agitator moving back and forth inside the tub.

When about 10 minutes had elapsed, Irene turned on another switch which started the wringer. This mechanism consisted of two rubber-coated rollers mounted on top of the machine. Irene found the end of one of the wet sheets and carefully inserted it between the two rollers, being sure her fingers didn't get caught in the rotating cylinders. She had had the unhappy experience of having her arm go through the wringer as a small girl. Fortunately, no permanent damage had been done.

As the corner of the sheet appeared on the other side of the rollers, Irene caught hold of it and guided it into the first tub of rinse water. The pressure of the rollers squeezed out much of the water from the fabric. Each piece was worked up and down in the rinse water by hand.

When the machine was empty, Barbara put in a second load of wash. Irene began taking the wash out of the first rinse tub and putting it through the wringer again into the second rinse tub. After all the items were in the final rinse, they were again taken out of the water and put through the wringer. This time, however, they were fluffed and dropped into a basket.

Irene took the finished wash outside and hung it on the washlines. The spring day was clear with a slight breeze. Irene was glad the weather was warm again. Handling damp clothing in the cold with numb fingers was not a pleasant task for her. She was also glad it wasn't raining so she didn't have to hang the wash on wooden racks inside.

Irene went back and forth from the wash house, carrying baskets of wash to the clotheslines. She helped her mother with the rinsing and wringing if a load was not finished. Some of the clothing made of no-iron fabrics was not put through the wringer but was hung to drip dry.

After five loads, the water in the machine was drained and refilled with fresh water. Barbara and Irene continued with five more loads.

The Honda engine on the washing machine was finally silenced a few minutes before ten o'clock. Barbara would have plenty of time to get the noon meal ready before the men came in from the fields.

Irene soon finished hanging the last of the wash. The first load she had hung was nearly dry. Most of the wash she would fold and put away, but some items would be set aside for later when she would heat up the "sad irons" on the stove and iron them.

By early afternoon, wash day was over at the Yoder home. The process would be repeated on a smaller scale on Friday and again the following Monday.

11.
Doing the Laundry

Nearly all Old Order Amish today use some type of washing machine. The most common variety is a Maytag wringer washer. This machine is usually powered by a two to three horsepower Honda or Briggs and Stratton engine, though in Lancaster County it is often operated on compressed air. Washing machine engines may have a pull starter or electric starter.

Even the ultra-conservative "Nebraska" and Swartzentruber Amish use motorized washing machines. However, the majority of Amish in Adams County, Indiana, do not. These Amish use only hand-operated machines—usually wringer washers converted from electric power. These machines are equipped with a lever which is moved back and forth to work the agitator. A hand crank operates the wringer. New machines of a similar design, called James Handwashers, are made by the Hutch and Such company of Topeka, Indiana, which also makes rabbit equipment.

Washing Machine History

Before the 1860s, washing machines were rare in North American homes. A variety of hand- and engine-operated devices came into use over the next 50 years, but as late as 1941 only half of all U.S. households had a washer. People without washing machines did their laundry by hand or, in urban areas, sent it to a commercial laundry. Automatic washers did not become available until the late 1930s, but they

A wringer washer equipped with a small gasoline engine is found in most Amish homes. In some cases, however, washing machines are powered by compressed air or hydraulic pumps.

increased rapidly in popularity after World War II.

The Maytag company began manufacturing a hand-powered washing machine in 1907. It offered an electric model in 1911 and a machine with a built-in gas engine in 1914. Factory-made gasoline engine machines were produced until 1952, and wringer washers were made until 1984. Used Maytags remain in great demand among the Amish, and some people make a business of refurbishing old machines.

The Speed Queen company still produces wringer washers. These are fitted with gasoline engines for Amish use.

Most Adams County, Indiana, washing machines are hand-powered, but this example shows how an ingenious farmer devised a horse-powered system. The large fly-wheel is attached to a shaft turned by the horse.

Amish laundry is hung on clotheslines all year, either outside or inside.

Drying

Although gas-operated dryers have been available for many years, they need electricity as an auxiliary power source. As far as this writer knows, no ingenious Amish person has been able to adapt a dryer for completely non-electric use.

Instead, the Amish hang their laundry on clotheslines year-round. In some communities, very long wash lines attached to large pulleys extend from house to barn. In Lancaster County, the clothesline often runs into the wash house. This allows the person doing the laundry to hang up the wash inside and convey it out through a door. In wet weather, clothes are placed on wooden racks inside or hung on lines in the basement or another room. A drying rack often is positioned above the cookstove.

Ironing

Because of the frequent use of "no-iron" synthetic materials, many Amish people do very little ironing. However, the delicate organdy head coverings of Amish women require careful pressing.

The old-style, solid-metal sad irons remain very much in use in Amish homes. These are heated on stoves in the traditional way. When the iron being used loses its heat, it is replaced by another that has been placed on the stove.

Although old sad irons are readily available and new ones of the old design are still being made, many Amish prefer discarded electric irons of the older, heavier type. These are devested of their cords and heated on stoves.

Self-heating irons also are in use among the Amish. These are variations on an old idea. In the 19th and early 20th centuries, irons that contained burning charcoal were common among the general North American population. Self-heating irons that burned gasoline, kerosene, or alcohol were available as early as the 1880s. Compressed air needed to be pumped into the gasoline irons.

Many different companies made these irons, but the Coleman Company, of lamp and lantern fame, dominated the market in its final phase. Coleman produced pressurized gas irons from 1925 to 1985. Most of the later models were sold in foreign countries and to the Amish. Many Amish people still use gas pressure irons, and some replacement parts are still available.

Gasoline-burning irons like these, as well as the old-style irons heated on a stove, are commonly used by the Amish.

In the 1980s, a butane-burning iron came on the scene. This iron was invented in England and marketed as a cordless iron for travelers.

The butane iron has proven much easier to use than the old gasoline irons and has found immediate popularity in some Amish communities. Butane irons are ignited electronically by a nine-volt battery and burn the same fuel as that used in some cigarette lighters. The irons are distributed by Lehman Hardware of Kidron, Ohio.

12.
How Do You Make Clothes Without An Electric Sewing Machine?

SHIPSHEWANA, Indiana—The November wind snapped at Mary Hochstetler's shawl as she tied her horse at the hitching rail beside Spector's. One of the Amish girls who worked in the store greeted her quietly as she stepped inside out of the wintry air. Several shoppers wearing bonnets and black shawls also smiled at her as she entered.

Mary went directly to the side of the store where bolts of fabric were lined on shelves and tables in preparation for the winter sewing season. She picked out blue chambray for work shirts for her husband, Jonas. A royal blue crepe would make a nice dress for 10-year-old Wilma and green teal for eight-year-old Martha. Mary chose blue denim for pants for Jonas and the boys, and white organdy for Sunday capes and aprons and for head coverings.

Calculating mentally how much fabric she needed for each item, Mary told the sales clerk how much of each material she wanted. Before she paid her bill, Mary added black stockings, thread, and buttons. She examined the store's selection of shoes but decided not to buy any today.

The next morning, after the children had gone to school, Mary got out the denim material for Jonas's and the boys' pants. She unfolded the fabric on the kitchen table and got the pants pattern out of a bureau drawer. Like all her patterns, these were homemade on brown paper. Most Amish clothing could not be bought in a store, and neither could plain patterns.

Trying to make use of every inch of fabric, Mary cut out the pieces to several pairs of pants and stacked them in piles according to size. Then she went to her sewing machine, which was situated in front of a window in the enclosed porch, where there was ample natural light. She lifted the lid of the cabinet, elevating the sewing machine head from a concealed, upside-down position to a ready-to-use, upright position. Finding the appropriate color of thread in a drawer of the cabinet, she pulled the fiber through the machine and finally through the needle. She placed a bobbin filled with the same color in its position beneath the plate under the pressure foot.

Mary put the first pieces under the needle and lowered the pressure foot to keep them in place. With her right hand she gave a quick downward jerk to the wheel on the side of the machine. With her right foot she rocked a wide pedal, called a treadle, just above floor level beneath the machine. This movement in turn set a large wheel turning beside the pedal. This large wheel was connected to the small wheel on the sewing machine by means of a long, thin leather belt. The motion was eventually transferred to the needle, which moved rapidly up and down.

Mary carefully guided the point around the perimeter of fabric, a quarter of an inch from the edge. Pedaling with her left foot when she tired, she moved rapidly through the first pair of pants. All that would be left for her to do after lunch was to hand-make the button holes and sew on the buttons.

As Mary folded the pants and laid them aside, the pile of clothes to be mended caught her eye. There were girls' dresses to be lengthened and hand-me-downs to be altered to fit younger wearers. The sewing machine would not be silent for long over the coming winter.

13.
Tailoring and Sewing

Though they make many of their own clothes, the Amish have not produced their own fabric since the middle of the 19th century. During the early 1800s, the industrial revolution made possible the mass production of textiles. Rural people who had previously made their own fabrics now found it cheaper and easier to buy them.

Apparently, few Amish resisted this transition. In 1862 Bishop David Beiler of Lancaster County, Pennsylvania, wrote of his regret that his people were no longer producing their own material.

From the beginning, however, the Amish have been selective in the fabric they buy. They have insisted that cloth be of solid colors and plain weave. Although practices vary according to community, a limited number of colors have been deemed acceptable for clothing. Blue is most popular, with brown, green, and gray also common. Brighter shades, such as purple and wine, can be found in some areas. However, pink, orange, and yellow are rare.

Typically, black is used for men's suites and women's bonnets and shawls. Men's Sunday shirts are usually white, as are women's headcoverings and capes and aprons in many communities.

Fabric Dealers

A number of dry goods stores specialize in fabrics preferred by the Amish. Spector's, which began in Mount Eaton, Ohio,

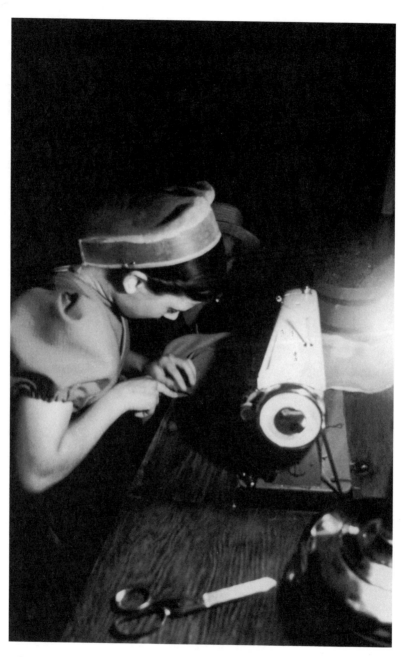

Although this sewing machine looks modern, it is powered by a foot treadle.

Many Amish women make most of their family's clothing on old-fashioned, foot-powered sewing machines. Considering the large size of Amish families, this is a big task.

in 1937, now has five branches in Ohio and Indiana. Gohn Brothers of Middlebury, Indiana, was founded in 1920. It does a large mail-order business. In addition to material, both stores sell ready-made items of Amish clothing, such as hats and shoes.

The Amish themselves operate dry goods stores in many communities. Some of these are confined to a room in a house, while others such as Zooks of Intercourse, Pennsylvania, fill a large building.

Sewing Machines

The Amish appear to have accepted sewing machines soon after the general population did. Introduced by Elias Howe and Isaac Singer in the 1840s, sewing machines were in common use among North Americans by the last quarter of the century.

Probably the last Amish to accept the use of machines were members of church districts in southern Adams County, Indiana. Even there, however, sewing machines have been permitted since the 1920s.

Most Amish do all of their sewing on foot-powered, treadle machines. The Bernina Company of Switzerland makes machines that are used by some Amish. These models look quite modern, except for their source of power.

Antique-looking machines made in Taiwan are used in some communities. Patterned after the old Singer, these models are more limited in function than the newer designs.

Still other Amish use machines that have been converted from electric to treadle power. Treadles from old sewing machines or new treadles made in an Amish shop in Lancaster County are used for these machines.

In some districts in the Lancaster area, sewing machines are run on compressed air. A foot pedal, very much like one on an electric machine, controls the amount of air moving the mechanism. Many Lancaster women who make quilts use machines of this sort for piecing and binding. (However, quilting and appliqueing are still done by hand.)

Specially-Made Articles

An Amish woman normally makes most of her family's clothing, following homemade patterns and traditional, prescribed styles. However, certain items of clothing that are difficult to produce are made by tailors within the community.

Men's suits and women's bonnets are often specially-made. Among the "Nebraska" and Swartzentruber Amish and in Lancaster County, women with particular skills make men's hats from strips of braided straw. Two Amish shops in the Lancaster area manufacture felt hats. In Somerset County, Pennsylvania, some Amish have started to make shoes.

14.
What Do You Do for Entertainment If You Don't Have TV?

MIDDLEFIELD, Ohio—Sylvia Miller had finished helping her mother with the supper dishes and settled down at the kitchen table with pen and paper. She wanted to write a letter to her favorite cousin, Rachel, who had moved from Geauga County, Ohio, to a new community in Michigan.

The other members of the Miller family were quietly occupied in the kitchen and living room of the farm house. The two rooms were connected by a wide doorway.

It was a cold winter evening and everyone wanted to stay close to the stoves. No one was off in another room or away at a meeting or social event. Nor was there a television, radio, or stereo to attract everyone's attention. Although they exchanged few words, the Millers enjoyed being together. There was something quietly reassuring about observing one another.

Sylvia looked up from her letter and glanced around the room, wondering what she could write about the other nine members of her family. She saw her parents, David and Amanda, sitting in their matching hickory rockers beneath the gas lamp. Her father read the cattle prices in the local paper, while her mother hand-sewed a dress.

In front of the wood-burning stove, four-year-old Benny played with a wooden farm set on the floor and made convincing imitations of the animal sounds. Eli, six, occasionally let out squeals of delight as he found a piece for the jigsaw puzzle he was assembling in the middle of the kitchen table. Close by, baby Miriam cooed softly to her stuffed toy.

Ten-year-old Suzy was absorbed in a magazine article, and eight-year-old Dan struggled through a library book that was a bit beyond his level. Thirteen-year-old Andy sat on the opposite end of the table from Sylvia, intently figuring the profits from his last sale of rabbits.

Sylvia thought of a few words to say about each person. When she had finished her letter, she got a songbook from the shelf and asked her sister Emma to help here learn a number they had heard for the first time in the singing last Sunday. At the end of the first three verses, Andy and Suzy joined in.

Dan and Eli, who had not yet learned to appreciate singing, started a game of Dutch Blitz™, which involved shouting and slapping cards on the table. The singers protested that the boys were too loud. A mild argument ensued. Father was trying to quell the fuss when he heard a knock at the door.

David's brother Abe had come with his wife, Lizzie, and their three children. Sylvia and her brothers and sisters were delighted to see their cousins. Abe explained that his family had been to visit Grandpa and Grandma Yoder and decided to stop for a visit.

While Amanda made a heaping bowl of popcorn for the guests, Sylvia and Emma listened to their cousin Betty tell of a neighbor's trip to the Natural History Museum in Cleveland. Sylvia wondered if she could talk her parents into such an outing.

Abe and David chatted about a building frolic that was being planned to construct a horse barn at Ray Mullet's. Amanda told Lizzie about a quilting to be held in the neighborhood the following week.

The visitors left a little after nine o'clock; it was high time for bed. David led the evening prayer as all knelt. Some of the children read for a few minutes in their bedrooms, but most were soon asleep. Days begin early on a farm.

15.
Social Activities

One of the most striking features of an Amish home is its quietness. There are few noisy appliances, and the blare of radios, televisions, and stereo systems is missing.

The Amish regard electronic entertainment as not only unnecessary but harmful. They do not want influences they view as corrupt to come into their homes via the airwaves or recorded material.

Despite the absence of entertainment devices, Amish life is far from boring. As a group, the Amish have much less idle time than other people. Most members can hardly imagine when they would have time to sit in front of a television.

Shared Work Projects

Because the Amish do not view work as drudgery, but as proper use of a person's energies, working together is considered as enjoyable as playing together. Many social activities revolve around work projects. The most famous of these are the barn raising and the quilting. there are also "frolics" to construct smaller buildings, clean schools, and help needy people.

Sisters in the same family often gather in one of the siblings' homes to sew, can, clean, or perform other domestic tasks. Farmers often share labor when threshing or filling a silo. A hearty meal usually goes along with the work.

Some shared projects have gone out of favor. Because corn is seldom picked from shocks, as it used to be, the old fashioned husking bee has become very rare among the Amish.

Barn raisings and other "work bees" are important social events which give people a chance to show their concern for other members of the community. By limiting mechanization, more opportunities to work together are created. The joy of sharing a task like sawing by hand (lower photo) would be missed if one-man chain saws were allowed.

The same is true of work bees to harvest rye straw for straw hats. This was a traditional activity in Lancaster County, Pennsylvania, but fell into decline when Amish hat-makers began using imported straw braid from China.

Holidays and Visits

In addition to work parties, the Amish socialize at a variety of other special occasions. Christmas celebrations include family dinners and the giving of gifts (though this is not emphasized as much as by other North Americans). Wedding festivities last all day and include much eating and singing. Fellowship meals follow each bi-weekly church service. Parents and children celebrate the last day of the school year with a picnic.

In addition, large groups of people gather for family reunions and meetings for occupational groups such as buggy-makers,

Amish youth enjoy vigorous physical activity as much as their modern counterparts do.

harness-makers, and pallet-makers. There are also large-scale teachers meetings and gatherings for handicapped people.

An important part of Amish life is informal visiting. Families often visit one another without advance notice, and it is common for unexpected guests to stay for a meal.

Even though they do not own cars, the Amish manage to travel widely. Groups often travel to distant Amish communities by bus, train, or hired van. Touring along the way is common.

Some Amish take trips purely for sightseeing, but this is discouraged by many leaders. Occasional family outings to a park, museum, or zoo are generally permitted.

Crafts and Games

Personal hobbies such as handcrafts and reading are encouraged in most Amish communities. Women and girls usually sew, quilt, knit, embroider, cross-stitch, or do other kinds of

needlework. People of all ages enjoy books, magazines, and newspapers. Some of these materials are produced by the Amish, but items from other sources can be found in most homes. Many Amish people use public libraries and bookmobiles.

Amish children, even adults, play various kinds of table games. One of these is Carrom, sometimes called Amish or Mennonite pool. This involves knocking small wooden disks into pockets in a playing board.

Checkers, chess, Parcheesi, and even Monopoly are among other popular table games. Card games such as Rook or Dutch Blitz are popular in some Amish circles but discouraged in others. Regular playing cards are generally taboo.

Like other young children, Amish youngsters enjoy such activities as hide and seek, tag, and jumping rope. Girls play with dolls. Instead of playing cops and robbers or cowboys and

Amish children are expected to help with farm work at an early age, but they still have time for fun. Without television and electronic games, Amish children must be more creative in their recreation than modern youngsters.

Singing is a favorite activity among the Amish. While traditional hymns are used for church, lighter gospel songs are permitted for other occasions.

Indians, Amish children act out farming practices or horse-and-buggy trips. Baler twine serves effectively as reins, and a wagon as a buggy. In addition, children may act out church services, taking turns as the preacher and congregation.

Summer activities for children include fishing and swimming, although mixed bathing groups of older boys and girls are usually discouraged. Teenagers and young adults play such games as volleyball and baseball. In some large settlements, youth groups have baseball teams that are more organized than church leaders would prefer.

In the winter, skating on farm ponds and sledding are popular activities. Boys often enjoy a vigorous game of hockey.

Singing Together

Though musical instruments are strongly discouraged among the Amish, some families enjoy singing together without accompaniment. This is especially common when doing work like washing dishes or processing food from the garden.

Singing also helps to pass the time on long trips.

Sunday evening singings are a regular activity for Amish youth. Typically, boys sit opposite girls at a long table. The majority of youth groups sing in German, but English is used in some communities. The tunes that are sung also vary from group to group. Youth in some communities sing only traditional slow tunes, while young people elsewhere use faster gospel and secular melodies.

16.
How Do You Communicate When You Don't Have a Phone?

JAMESPORT, Missouri—Lydia Mast walked a quarter of a mile down the gravel lane. When she arrived at the mailbox, she lifted the lid eagerly. She could hardly believe how much mail she saw. There was a small cardboard box, a newspaper, a magazine, and several letters.

The 18-year-old hurriedly leafed through the letters and found one addressed to her. The handwriting was unfamiliar and there was no return address. When it dawned on her that the writing looked masculine, she caught her breath and tore open the envelope. Just as she thought, Daniel Troyer was asking to take her home from the singing on Sunday night.

Before Lydia realized it, she had walked back to the house and had not even looked at the other mail. Eight-year-old Miriam grabbed the Family Life magazine from her hands. As Miriam was trying to find the children's section, 11-year-old Joe swooped in and grabbed the precious periodical.

A scream of protest brought Mother Mast to the

door. After seeing that the magazine was returned to Miriam, Alice asked Lydia what else was in the mail. Lydia blushed, but her mother's attention was diverted by a letter from her sister Ruth, who lied in Wisconsin. All of Alice's other work waited until she had read the latest news from her far-off sibling.

About this time, 15-year-old Daniel Mast emerged from the barn and asked if there was anything for him. Lydia handed him the box. His eyes grew very big, and he began tearing at the corners of the stubborn tape which sealed the cardboard. Inside was a book on horse training. Daniel walked off, looking excitedly through the pages.

While the other Masts were engrossed in their mail, a cloud of dust appeared at the end of the lane. Father Mast pulled into the farm yard in his spring wagon. He had gone to town to use the public phone. One of his Belgian work horses was sick, and a vet needed to be summoned.

Alice gave her husband a letter. Sam was puzzled by the postmark from upstate New York. He opened the envelope and found a letter from cousin Levi Hershberger. Levi was coming to visit the Masts in May. He and his family were going to a wedding in another part of Missouri.

Sam turned his attention to the Budget newspaper and glanced at the many letters from Amish communities all over North America. The headline from his former home area of Dover, Delaware, caught his eye.

Sam carried the paper into the house and put it

and Levi's letter away for a more leisurely hour. There was much work to be done, but the mail would provide many enjoyable moments later.

17.
Staying In Touch

Telephones are not allowed in the home in most Old Order Amish communities. The Amish believe that phones, like cars, are not wrong in themselves, but that easy access to them is destructive to the family and church.

Telephone calls intrude on the life of a family and often waste time, the Amish believe. Moreover, phones create a symbolic link to the world in the same way that electric lines do, and they invite many temptations that could otherwise be avoided.

Permissible Uses of Phones

Although having a phone at home is prohibited, most groups allow limited use of Alexander Graham Bell's invention. Amish people use pay phones. In addition, they make calls on the phones of non-Amish neighbors, although church leaders have admonished that this be restricted to emergencies, such as calling a doctor or veterinarian, or giving a death notice.

Some neighbors have installed phones in their garages especially for the Amish to use. Each user keeps track of long distance calls and pays the owner of the phone.

In most Amish settlements, a non-Amish person or organization has agreed to receive emergency calls, especially death notices. Many of these contact people are funeral directors. Others operate taxi services for the Amish; some are simply owners of local businesses, or even work for the police department.

Though telephones are forbidden in the home in most Amish communities, neighborhood phones placed in a shed or barn are widely permitted (top). The bill is shared and long-distance calls are listed in a notebook. The use of public telephones (bottom) is allowed by every Amish group.

This neighborhood phone booth is located in Ohio. In some Amish communities, telephones are permitted in places of business or in sheds adjacent to shops.

In a number of communities, several Amish families share a phone in a centrally-located shed or at an Amish school. Thefts of these community phones were common in Holmes County, Ohio, for a time. The solution was to put locks on the phone sheds and issue keys to each subscriber.

Business Phones

For people in business, living without a home phone poses special difficulties. Because of this, some districts in Lancaster County, Pennsylvania, and Geauga County, Ohio, allow telephones for members who have home businesses. It is usually required that these phones be in a separate shed or building, however, not in the house or shop.

Some Amish businesses have telephone numbers listed in phone books and in advertising. In certain of these cases, amplified bells for incoming calls are allowed.

A few Amish groups permit farmers who do not operate other businesses to have phones in their barns or outbuildings. A handful of groups allow telephones in the home.

Because the Amish have few other means of communication, the arrival of the mail is an important event.

Correspondence by Mail

The Amish rely heavily on the U.S. and Canadian postal services. Personal communications and business transactions that many people would handle by phone are carried out through the mail by the Amish.

Many Amish participate in circle letters, in which people of similar interests, occupations, or situations (such as widows, teachers, or harness-makers) correspond with one another.

An Amish person probably writes more letters than the average North American. Amish families typically subscribe to several newspapers and magazines.

Typically, a person receives a packet containing letters from each person in the circle. The receiver takes out the portion he or she had written for the last round and adds a new letter, before sending the whole batch to the next person.

Newspapers and Magazines

Two weekly newspapers report news from Amish communities throughout North America. The older of these is the *Budget*, which was established in 1890 in Sugarcreek, Ohio. This started out as a local newspaper, but soon became wider in scope because of its inclusion of letters from far-flung Amish and Mennonite communities.

The letters contained in the *Budget* are of a very folksy nature and include reports on weather, visits, illnesses, accidents, and church services, as well as births, deaths, and marriages. Little news of national importance is mentioned except that which directly affects the Amish and other plain people.

Die Botschaft (German for "The Message") is published in Lancaster, Pennsylvania, and is almost identical to the *Budget*. Contrary to what its name might suggest, nearly all its contents are in English.

Die Botschaft was started in 1975 for those who wanted a paper with letters from only horse-and-buggy groups. The *Budget* contains material from both horse-and-buggy and other plain groups. Some writers send duplicate letters to both papers.

The *Diary* is a monthly Amish magazine. It is similar to the *Budget* and *Die Botschaft*, except that it categorizes news according to subject (births, deaths, marriages, etc.) and includes serial stories and historical articles.

Pathway Publishers of Aylmer, Ontario, produces three magazines very popular in many Old Order communities. The largest magazine by circulation is *Family Life*, a general interest publication containing religious articles and other material relating to the Old Order way of life. *Young Companion* focuses on youth, while *Blackboard Bulletin* addresses issues important to Amish schools and teachers.

18.
How Do You Get Around Without a Car?

HAZLETON, Iowa—John Gingerich hurried to the barn, putting on his coat and hat as he went and chewing the last bite of an apple. Dad said he must make haste if he wanted to be on time.

John got the family driving horse, Polly, from her stall. He placed the harness on Polly's back and led the mare outside to the buggy shed. Next year when he was 16, he would have a horse of his own, John thought to himself.

John pulled out the two-seated black vehicle by the long shafts that extended from the front axle. Carefully, he moved the buggy forward until Polly was between the shafts. He inserted the end of each into the heavy leather loops positioned on the horse's side.

After making all the other necessary connections between horse and vehicle, he fed the reins through the front of the buggy. John climbed into the buggy and fastened down the side of the curtain to keep out the October air. Grasping the reins, he clicked with his mouth to signal the horse to go forward.

The grinding of the steel wheels and clopping of the horse's hooves rose in pitch as John turned from the gravel back road to the blacktopped road to town. A pickup truck whizzed by suddenly—the first motor vehicle John had met since leaving home. A large orange triangle on the back of the buggy warned motorists of the horse-drawn vehicle's presence.

In the town of Hazleton, John pulled into the parking lot of a convenience store and tied his horse to a hitching rack beside another horse and buggy. Inside the store he saw a friend, Andy Helmuth, sitting at one of the booths by the snack bar.

"Picking up someone for the wedding?" Andy called out.

"Yep. My Uncle Abe and Aunt Sarah from Canada are supposed to be here," John drawled. "Who are you waiting for?"

"My brother and sister-in-law from Bowling Green, Missouri," Andy replied.

The two boys sipped soft drinks and discussed who they expected to see at the wedding. It was four-thirty when they heard the roar of a diesel engine.

An elderly Amish couple appeared at the door of the bus, but neither John nor Andy knew them. The white-bearded man shook hands with the boys and introduced himself as Noah Miller. John guessed from his clothes that he was from Kalona, near Iowa City. The Amish from that community were not as conservative as those in the Hazleton area.

A similarly dressed younger couple got off the bus, and they and the Millers went to a gray van parked nearby. They had arranged to be met by one of the local people who provided transportation for the Amish.

The middle-aged couple disembarking next greeted John enthusiastically. John helped his aunt and uncle carry their few items of luggage to the buggy. They had a pleasant time visiting during the hour it took to travel eight miles to John's home. Abe and Sarah explained that they had taken the train from Ingersoll, Ontario, to Chicago. they had spent the night in the city before catching the bus to Iowa.

As John pulled into his family's driveway, he saw a long blue van that had Minnesota plates. A man who was "English"—the Amish term for people outside the group—sat behind the wheel. A tall thin Amish man was emerging from the sliding door.

"It's Uncle Joe!" John exclaimed.

Abe and Sarah greeted Joe and his family warmly. Joe explained that they had hired a van and driver to bring the whole family from their home in southern Minnesota. It was much cheaper than taking the bus. Besides, after the wedding they wanted to go on to southern Iowa to visit other relatives.

It was a joyous time at the Gingerich home that evening. Everyone wondered who else they might see at the wedding.

19.
Transportation

The most obvious difference between the Amish and the larger society, next to clothing, is mode of transportation. In an era dominated by the automobile, the use of horse-drawn vehicles seems extremely anachronistic.

When automobiles were first introduced, they were neither practical nor reliable. The Amish and many other people saw them as a plaything of the rich.

Around the time of the First World War, however, it became clear that the motor car would replace the horse and buggy as the usual means of transportation. But the Amish remained skeptical that adopting cars was in their best interest.

Over the years, as the impact of the auto has become more obvious, Amish objections have only grown stronger. Foremost is the belief that car ownership is a disintegrating force on family, church, and community. Car owners tend to be away from home too much, the Amish believe, and vehicles make the community more scattered and less cohesive.

Convenient transportation tends to make it easier to yield to temptation, the Amish say. With a car, you can go wherever you want, whenever you want. This is especially harmful to young people.

The Amish point out further that cars are often objects of pride and can become status symbols. The features of style, speed, comfort, and convenience promoted by car manufacturers are in direct opposition to the Amish values of nonconformity, simplicity, self-denial, and humility. Having such a powerful machine tends to make people feel more important than they ought to, some Amish say.

Cars usually have radios and require insurance—both prohibited by the Ordnung (Amish rules and regulations). In addition, the Amish believe that automobile travel is more dangerous than horse-and-buggy transportation.

Many people assume that the Amish forbid all use of motor vehicles. This has never been true. In the days before the auto age, the Amish did not object to using public transportation—trains, trolleys, stage coaches, and ships. When buses came along, the Amish did not forbid riding on them, either. (Air travel, however, is proscribed by nearly all Old Order Amish groups, except in extreme emergencies.)

The use of mechanical conveyances was not and is not the issue. What the Amish do not want is ready access to a motor

Each Amish community has a distinctive style of vehicle. In the Milverton settlement in Ontario, only open vehicles are used.

vehicle. By forbidding car ownership, the harmful effects of cars can largely be avoided. To reinforce this rule, all driving of cars is also prohibited.

As public transportation systems in the United States have deteriorated, the Amish have had to rely more and more on

Horse-drawn vehicles serve many different functions. A Mifflin County, Pennsylvania, farmer hauls his pigs to market in a spring wagon (top), while a New Wilmington, Pennsylvania, farmer picks up supplies in his family carriage (bottom).

Foot-powered scooters are distinctive to Lancaster County Amish. Bicycles are permitted in a few communities, but most Amish forbid them.

hired autos and vans. In most Amish communities, several non-Amish people provide taxi services. However, Amish leaders caution against using this type of transportation too much. This warning, along with the expense of hired cars and drivers, limits taxi use for most Amish.

The manufacture of horse-drawn vehicles is still very much alive in Amish communities. All kinds of buggies, carriages, wagons, and carts are hand crafted in dozens of Amish shops. Each community has its own distinctive style of vehicles.

Often a shop specializes in a particular phase of buggy making. This is especially true of such parts as wheels, shafts, springs, and axles. In addition to the vehicles themselves, har-

Changes in Technology in One Amish Community
Partridge, Kansas

1883   Settlement started.

1935   Combines and tractors with steel wheels permitted.

early 1940s   Rubber tread bolted on steel tractor wheels permitted.

mid-1940s   Pneumatic tractor tires permitted on front of tractor.

1948   Pneumatic tractor tires permitted on back of tractor.

early 1950s   Small tractors with trailers serve as transportation during the week. Buggies are still used on Sunday. Some businessmen are allowed to have pickup trucks. A few people convert passenger cars into makeshift pickups. Some boys in alternate service are permitted to drive cars.

1954   Electricity and telephones are permitted. Electricity is originally limited for farm use and washing, ironing, and lighting in the house.

1958   The church divides into Beachy Amish (two-thirds) and Old Order Amish (one-third). The Beachy Amish permit full use of cars and electricity. The Old Order forbid all use of cars.

From *History and Change of the Amish of Reno County, Kansas* by David Wagler.

Restrictions on tractor use vary a great deal among Amish communities. The Holmes County, Ohio, tractor pictured above has rubber tread bolted to steel wheels. Some Amish groups allow no rubber on the wheels, while a few permit pneumatic tires. The most conservative groups do not allow any use of tractors.

nesses necessary for horse-drawn transportation are made in Amish shops.

For driving purposes, the Amish prefer standardbred horses. Few of these animals are raised by the Amish. Instead, the majority are horses bred for harness racing. Animals that are not fast enough for the track or that have been retired are quite adequate for Amish use. The Amish have no objection to using these horses, even though the animals were raised for a purpose of which the Amish disapprove.

In some communities, bicycles are frequently used. This is true of many districts in the Holmes County, Ohio; LaGrange County, Indiana; and Arthur, Illinois, settlements. In Geauga County, Ohio, as well as the more conservative districts in Holmes County and elsewhere, bicycles are not allowed. In Lancaster County, Pennsylvania, bicycles are officially forbidden, but various kinds of foot-powered scooters have been permitted for many years.

Those Amish that forbid bikes believe that this form of transportation offers too much mobility to the rider.

20.
How Can You Farm Without a Tractor?

NORWICH, Ontario—Daniel Shetler guided his team of horses into position as he sat on the mower and tightly grasped the reins. He lowered the long jagged sickle bar into the alfalfa, then put the mower into gear and motioned the horses forward. There was no engine on this machine; the wheels provided the motion which sent the blades of the mower moving back and forth. This source of power was known as "ground drive."

With a clippity-clippity sound, the toothed arm of the mower scissored off the vegetation. The sickle bar created a green wave as it moved across the field.

The morning was bright, and Daniel hoped that the June sun would continue shining until the hay could be gathered into the barn. He made steady progress as he went around and around a four-acre section of the field. When he finished mowing, he raised the sickle bar into its vertical position and drove the horses back to the barn. Now the hay would be given a chance to dry.

In the afternoon Daniel took his team to another field and cultivated corn.

The next morning Daniel hitched a tedder to his team and returned to the hay field. The tedder was a two-wheeled implement with a series of two-tined forks arranged in an uneven line across the back of the machine. Like the mower, it had no motor.

When Daniel drove this device across the cut alfalfa, the forks lifted the hay and fluffed it. This action ensured faster and more even drying. It was essential that the hay not be too wet, or it would mold in the barn or even catch fire through spontaneous combustion. But sometimes, on days that were very hot and low in humidity, the hay could dry without tedding.

Daniel spent the afternoon cutting another four-acre section of hay. The following morning, he hitched his team to the side delivery rake and returned to the section he had tedded. On each pass through the field, rotating bars lined with rod-like tines swiftly gathered the blanket of vegetation into long, loose ridges called windrows.

After the Shetlers finished the noon meal, 17-year-old Mary and 13-year-old Levi rode along with Daniel on a large flat-bedded wagon with a hay loader attached to the end. This ground-driven, unmotorized contraption extended the width of the wagon and towered above it at roughly a 45-degree angle.

At the beginning of the first windrow, Mary took the reins. Daniel put the loader in gear and the tines of a rotating cylinder began picking up the hay as the horses walked on either side of the row. A series of moving arms lined with long tines took the hay up a wide incline and dropped it into the wagon.

Daniel and Levi quickly forked the hay to the

front of the wagon. As the loader moved through the field, the hay piled up higher and higher. Soon father and son were perched far above the wagon bed. They were kept busy distributing the hay evenly, so that the wagon would not become unbalanced and tip.

When the bed was nearly full, Daniel's married son, Noah, who lived on a neighboring farm, brought a second wagon to the field. Daniel and his sons unhooked the loader from the first wagon and attached it to the empty one.

Noah drove the load of hay back to the barn and cautiously entered the center door at the top of the earthen slope. He halted the horses beneath the large jaws of an iron grappling device attached to a rope. Noah climbed to the top of the load and positioned the fork on top of the stack.

The fork was connected by rope to the hay carrier, a wheeled device attached to a metal rack running the length of the barn. The rope continued through pulleys and out the front of the barn, where it was attached to another team of horses.

Noah shouted to his 14-year-old sister, Miriam, to lead the horses away from the barn. This elevated a load of hay off the wagon. When the load was raised all the way to the top, it was pulled to one side of the barn on a track.

Noah's cousin Chris was in the hay mow of the barn. He yelled to Miriam when the load was in the right position. Noah pulled another rope attached to the fork, releasing the hay. Miriam backed up the horses, and Noah pulled the fork and hay carrier back to the middle of the barn by the release rope.

It took several loads to empty the wagon. After each load was released, Chris busily forked the hay into the corners of the mow.

When the wagon was emptied, Noah drove it back to the field to exchange with a full wagon. This process continued through the afternoon. Unless there was rain, the same steps of mowing, tedding, raking, and loading would be continued for several days until all 12 acres of alfalfa were harvested.

21.
Amish Agriculture

Until the advent of tractor farming, the differences between Amish farming methods and those of the large society were not great. Although perhaps with some hesitation, the Amish generally adjusted to technological advancements on the farm in the 19th and early 20th centuries. When horses replaced oxen as the draft animals of choice, the Amish adapted. Similarly, the Amish accepted the use of mechanical hay loaders, grain binders, and threshing machines, and even steam-powered equipment.

Shift from Horses to Tractors

Only in the years immediately after World War II did Amish farming practices begin to diverge widely from those of the surrounding society. Though cars in the United States had almost completely replaced horses for transportation by 1930, it was not until the 1950s that the transition from draft horses to tractors on the farm was complete. According to 1940 Pennsylvania statistics, for example, approximately 25 percent of all farmers in the state had horses but no tractors, 30 percent had both horses and tractors, and only 20 percent had tractors but no horses. Twenty-five percent had neither tractors nor horses.

After World War II the shift to tractors rapidly gained momentum, thanks in part to an intense advertising campaign by agricultural agencies and farm implement manufacturers. By 1960, horse power for agriculture was largely a memory—except among the Amish.

*These Ohio Amish farmers still gather loose, rather than baled, hay.
Many Amish now use horse-drawn, motorized balers.*

Advantages of Farming with Horses

The Amish had both practical and religious reasons to be leery of the tractor. Although tractors offered speed, power, and convenience, horses were far less expensive for daily use. Fuel for tractors had to be purchased, while feed for horses could be grown on the land. In contrast to the noxious exhaust produced by tractors, waste matter from horses could be returned to the soil for its betterment. Moreover, horses reproduced themselves, while worn-out tractors had to be replaced at high cost.

In addition, the Amish found that horses frequently outperformed tractors in adverse conditions, such as mud or snow. Horse farmers often could start plowing in the spring when the ground was still too soft for tractors. Along with this, the Amish believed that the heavy weight of tractors compacted the soil in harmful ways.

Threat to Amish Values

Most importantly, the Amish saw tractor farming as a threat to their way of life. Increased mechanization on the farm

Early in the 20th century, Amish leaders decided that the use of tractors in the filed was detrimental to the Amish way of life.

American Farm Technology History Compared to Current Amish Farm Technology

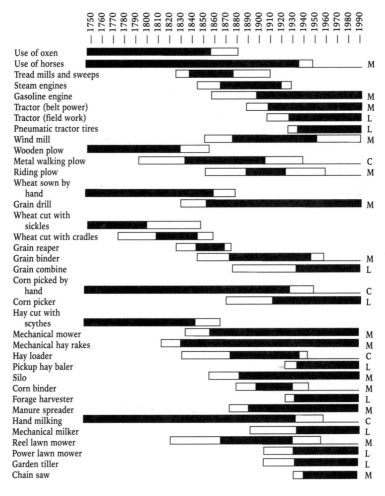

Legend

☐	Period of increasing or declining use
■	Period of common use
—	Continuing use among Amish
O	Used by few if any Amish
C	Used by the more conservative Amish
L	Used by the more liberal Amish
M	Used by the majority of the Amish
E	Used by the small minority of Amish who allow electricity

This old-style hay loader is used by "Nebraska" Amish men in central Pennsylvania.

offered fewer opportunities for farmers to cooperate in joint work projects such as threshing or filling silos. Also, there was less work for children to do. This meant fewer opportunities for children to learn the value of hard work and more chances for them to engage in destructive behavior.

To the Amish, the indiscriminate use of tractors was and continues to be a symbol of an approach to farming that is directly opposed to their values. Mechanized farming of large acreages dominated by a single crop may be financially lucrative in the short run, the Amish say, but it does long-term damage to the land. Some agricultural experts agree. These authorities have studied the Amish practices of diversification and rotation of crops, as well as the use of manure for fertilizer, and have found these methods superior to many modern farming techniques.

In addition to benefiting the environment, the Amish approach to agriculture contributes to the economic stability of farmers by avoiding the need for heavy borrowing. The Amish see folly in the cycle which requires larger and more expensive machines to maintain ever-larger acreages. The agricultural crisis of the 1980s, in which thousands of farmers suffered financial failure, seems to support the Old Order view.

The most conservative Amish still pick corn by hand. This Ohio farmer gleans corn from a neighbor's machine-picked field.

Although Amish farmers were not immune from the problems around them, a relatively small number went under.

The small farms operated by the Amish (usually on less than 100 acres) seldom produce great wealth for their owners. In most cases, however, they provide a modest but comfortable living. This is all the Amish really want.

Types of Horses Used

On Amish farms, horses pull plows and do much of the heavy work. The large work or draft animals used on Amish farms are typically Belgians, Percherons, or some mixture of these or other strains. Belgians are currently the most popular breed of draft horse in America. As the name implies, this strain originated in Belgium. Originally, several color combinations were found among the breed, but now sorrels with white manes and tails predominate.

Percherons are also common on Amish farms. Most of these animals are either black or gray. This breed had its beginnings in the old French province of Perche and was the most popular work horse in the United States from the 1880s to the 1930s.

In recent years, the Percheron has been regaining some of its past favor. Although these animals are a little smaller than Belgians, some horse experts say they have a better disposition and more endurance.

Although some Amish farmers raise registered purebred work horses, many of these are sold to non-Amish people. Amish farmers generally care only that their horses be good workers and are hesitant to pay the price for a horse of unmixed lineage.

In some communities, registered horses are not allowed. The Amish in these settlements believe that owning such animals is a sign of extravagance and pride.

Use of Mules

In Lancaster County, Pennsylvania, and settlements originating from there, many Amish farmers use mules. Some farmers have both horses and mules and may mix the teams.

Mules are a sterile hybrid from a male donkey, or jack, and a female horse. Most mules used by the Lancaster Amish are bred by non-Amish in Missouri, Tennessee, and Kentucky and shipped to horse sales in the county.

Farmers who prefer mules claim that the animals have more endurance than horses and are friendlier, more intelligent, and easier to train. The smaller feet of mules are also said to be less likely to damage crops. On the other side, some Amish have forbidden the use of mules, viewing them the product of a union that is unnatural and therefore contrary to God's will.

Farm Implements

In the years immediately after the transition to tractor farming in the larger world, the Amish were able to find an abundance of discarded horse-farming implements. Much of this equipment was still in use in the 1980s, even though it was more than thirty years old. Machinery of this sort has become increasingly scarce, however, as the Amish population continues to grow and old implements wear out.

To meet the farm equipment needs of their community many Amish have gone into the implement repair business. Some Amish shops purchase hard-to-find replacement parts from the stocks of large companies. Others have begun manufacturing new components for old machinery.

A number of Amish-owned companies make not only parts but complete implements. Many types of plows are made in Amish shops. New horse-drawn cultivators and harrows are produced, along with several kinds of manure spreaders and farm wagons.

Amish businesses also manufacture steel wheels, hitch carts and other devices to adapt modern equipment for Amish use. Also know as the fore truck, the hitch cart is a two-wheeled vehicle that can be hitched to a team of horses. Plows, manure spreaders, side delivery hay rakes, and a host of other tractor implements can then be attached to the cart.

Engines and Motorized Equipment

Very much contrary to the idea that the Amish still farm as their ancestors did two hundred years ago is their use of internal combustion engines. Developed in the middle of the 19th century, gasoline engines began to gain wide acceptance in the larger society in the 1890s. By the 1930s, they had replaced steam engines as the leading source of power for farm machines.

Today only a small minority of Amish prohibit all use of gasoline or diesel engines. Some groups, however, use engines only to provide belt power for stationary devices such as threshing machines, ensilage cutters, and hand-fed hay balers. Many other groups require that motorized equipment be pulled by horses rather than self-propelled. Among the horse-

Horse farmers have been able to adapt equipment meant for tractors by using two-wheeled "hitch carts," shown here attached to a manure spreader.

drawn motorized implements used by these Amish are corn pickers; field hay balers that pick up hay from the ground; hay conditioners, also called crimpers, which speed the drying time after hay is cut; and flair choppers, which shred corn stubble in the field after corn has been picked.

Many pieces of motorized farm equipment are made to be attached to the power take-off of a tractor. This is a rotating shaft in the rear of the tractor which is powered by the tractor engine but individually controlled. Often, the Amish connect a gasoline or diesel engine to the shaft that would ordinarily be attached to the power take-off.

Grain Binders and Corn Binders

Some motorized farm equipment has not been adapted for Amish use. Few Amish use horse-drawn combines to harvest grain. Instead, the old style grain binders are employed to cut the grain and tie it in bundles, and threshing machines separate the straw, chaff, and grain.

Most modern farmers use forage harvesters to chop standing corn into ensilage. In this method the corn is chopped and blown into a wagon as the apparatus is pulled through the field. Then the ensilage wagon is unloaded into the silo by means of a blower.

By contrast, most Amish use corn binders which cut the corn stalks and bind them into bundles. These bundles are carried by wagon and fed into the ensilage cutter, which chops that corn into small pieces and blows it into the silo.

Ground-Driven Machinery

Often, grain binders and corn binders are ground-driven—that is, powered by the motion of one of the wheels of the machine. The same is true of mowers used for harvesting hay.

Amish farmers in Allen and Daviess counties in Indiana have found that hay balers, corn pickers, and other equipment designed to be powered by engines or a tractor's power take-

In Lancaster County, Pennsylvania, motorized devices such as this mower and hay conditioner are pulled by horses.

Although grain binders like this have not been manufactured since the 1950s, the Amish keep them in running condition.

off can be converted to ground drive. Differentials and transmissions from used trucks are employed to transfer power from a broad "bull wheel" to the mechanism of a machine. Devices run in this way require extra horses to pull; as many as eight horses are needed to pull a ground-driven corn picker.

In Lancaster County, some Amish have developed a ground-driven cart that can be attached to various machines.

Permissible Uses of Tractors

Despite their objections to mechanized agriculture, most Amish groups allow limited use of tractors. Usually these are used only for belt power. Occasionally, heavy pulling work is allowed, but not field work such as plowing.

Most groups require that tractors have steel wheels. Pneumatic, rubber tires are not allowed, although rubber tread cut from tires is often bolted to steel wheels in order to prevent tearing up the pavement on public roads.

The rule against pneumatic tires is a measurement to prevent tractors from being used for transportation, as a substitute for automobiles. Without air tires, tractors are not capable of achieving high speeds or smooth rides. Those Amish who do not allow self-propelled tractors are providing a further margin of safety between themselves and cars.

Lawn and Garden Equipment

In many communities, the Amish have become known for their carefully manicured lawns and well-kept gardens. Most Amish people till their gardens by hand or with horse-drawn implements, but in some large settlements motorized rototillers have been accepted. Rotary power mowers and motorized line trimmers to cut weeds are also the norm in some Amish settlements.

In the more conservative districts, only non-motorized lawn mowers are permitted. Push mowers are the general rule in Lancaster County, although some districts have begun to permit power mowers and line trimmers. In a number of communities, including Lancaster and Geauga County, Ohio, some Amish use reel mowers pulled by a pony.

The very conservative Swartzentruber Amish permit only push mowers and restrict the use of these devices to fenced-in yards. The rest of the farmstead is not to be mowed.

The "Nebraska" Amish of central Pennsylvania and some of

The Amish community of Kalona, Iowa, permits tractors for field work, but their use is limited by allowing only steel wheels.

120

Reel-type push mowers are still manufactured for the general public, so they are easily obtained by those Amish who do not permit power mowers.

the Amish in Adams County, Indiana, use no mowers at all. The grass around their houses is trimmed by grazing animals or with a scythe or sickle.

22.
How Can You Run a Dairy Farm Without Electricity?

PARADISE, Pennsylvania—Milking time at the Fisher farm began immediately after the silent prayer at the end of the evening meal. Isaac, the father, pushed the button in the milk house that started the diesel engine. Eight-year-old John, the younger of the Fisher boys, began sanitizing the milker apparatus, while his 17-year-old brother, Reuben, herded the 26 Holstein cows into their places in the barn.

The Fishers' dairy operation, like those of most Amish farmers in southeastern Pennsylvania, was considerably less mechanized than the simplest non-Amish farms. Yet it was far removed from the days when milking was done by hand and the product shipped in metal cans.

Isaac still remembered that time, before vacuum milking machines, bulk storage tanks and battery-powered devices to stir the milk. The Amish had voluntarily accepted mechanical milkers in the 1950s, Isaac recalled. Then, in the 1960s, dairies began requiring refrigerated tanks with an agitator.

Amish leaders had opposed the use of electric generators necessary for the new system, but the milk companies refused to budge.

In Isaac's community, the Amish farmers gave in. In other areas, including some parts of Ohio, they clung to the old ways. This meant that they had to sell their milk at a much lower price to cheese producers that did not insist on the new methods. Isaac had friends who had left the dairy business because of the drop in prices. Some of these men had to find work in factories.

I'm glad I didn't have to do that, Isaac thought to himself, as he watched his youngest son place the stainless steel parts of the milker apparatus in the wash tub. John cleaned each item inside and out, and Isaac scrubbed the inside of the milk tank. The tank was washed out every other day, after the milk truck had emptied it. Cleanliness was imperative. The purer the milk, the higher its price. Impure milk might be rejected altogether.

With little prodding from Reuben, the black and white cows arranged themselves in two long rows running the length of the barn. Each animal knew where she belonged. Isaac chained the cows to metal stanchions through which their heads protruded. The animals munched grain provided in troughs in front of them.

After seeing that his sons had their tasks under control, Isaac made his way to the harness shop to work there. Reuben fetched the milkers his brother had washed. Each consisted of a container with a detachable lid from which a hose branched into four rubber tentacles. These ended in steel cylindrical cups.

Reuben plugged a long hose attached to the milker lid into a valve in a pipe above the row of cows. He placed the milker unit beside the first cow and stooped to wash the udder with disinfectant. Then he put each of the four cups on the cow. Suction held the rubber-lined cups in place and drew milk with a pulsating rhythm.

Reuben attached the other two units to two other cows. A small glass container at the juncture of the four tentacles allowed him to see when the milk was flowing. When milk from the first cow stopped, he dipped each of the animal's teats in a jar of solution. This was supposed to help prevent the disease mastitis.

Criss-crossing between the two rows of cows, Reuben drained each animal and poured its white liquid into a stainless steel bucket. Unlike non-Amish dairy farmers, the Fishers did not have a system that conveyed milk directly to the bulk tank. So Reuben periodically took full buckets of milk to the milk house, where he poured them into large funnels on top of the tank.

While the cows were being milked, John went to the upper floor of the barn and threw down bales of hay through a hole in the barn floor. He separated the bales into sections, loaded them into a wheelbarrow and distributed them to the cows.

John also threw down bales of corn fodder for bedding. This was distributed in the pens of "dry cows" (those not giving milk) and "heifers" (young cows that had not yet given birth).

Reuben removed the milker from the last cow at six forty-five. But the boys' work was not over. Reuben needed to climb into the silo and shovel down chopped, brown vegetation for the cows to eat. John needed to clean the milkers a second time and wash the milk house floor.

In addition, Isaac would return to distribute shovelfuls of peanut hulls as bedding for the cows. He would check the gutters in the floor to see if they needed to be cleaned of manure. If so, the next day a horse would drag a metal device through the gutter and push the manure into a hole in the floor.

The cows were now ready for the night. In less than 12 hours, the evening's work would be repeated at the six a.m. milking.

23.
Milk and Cheese Production

In most Amish communities the milk check is an important part of a farmer's income. But dairying is not a particularly old occupation. Until the 1870s, North Americans drank little milk. Before this time most milk was made into butter and cheese, primarily because adequate refrigeration for the liquid was not widely available. The use of milk increased rapidly after 1900, and many Amish farmers developed dairy herds in response.

Farmers in many Amish communities do all their milking by hand. In such settlements as Geauga County, Ohio, and Adams County, Indiana, virtually all milking is done in this way. The same holds true for a large percentage of districts in Holmes County, Ohio, and LaGrange County, Indiana.

Where hand milking is still practiced, the whole family usually takes part in the morning and evening ritual. Every family member who is able milks several cows. As the family grows, so does the herd of cows.

Mechanical Milkers

Milking machines were introduced in 1905. Farmers were slow to adopt milkers, however, and in 1950 only 59 percent of all U.S. dairy farms had such machines. (An even lower percentage of farms that had cows but were not primarily dairy operations used milkers at this time.)

More than half of all Old Order Amish dairy farmers milk their cows by hand.

The Amish in Lancaster County, Pennsylvania, began using milkers relatively early, in the 1950s. Milking machines later were permitted in Arthur, Illinois; Nappanee, Indiana; and some districts in LaGrange County and Holmes County.

Amish farms that use machines typically suction milk into individual buckets for each milker, rather than send it through pipes to the storage tank, as in most modern dairies.

The most conservative Amish groups still store milk in old-style metal cans. The milk cans are placed in troughs of flowing water for cooling.

Buyers of Grade A milk in most states require that milk be refrigerated at lower temperatures than are possible with water cooling. Thus, the Amish who insist on maintaining the water cooling method are forced to sell their milk to cheese manufacturers as Grade B product. This explains the presence of large cheese plants in many Amish communities.

In some districts in Ohio and Indiana, farmers comply with buyers' requirements by putting their milk cans in mechanically refrigerated coolers run by diesel engines. Other Amish

In the most traditional Amish communities, milk is still stored in cans and cooled by flowing water. This milk must be used for making cheese, because Grade A milk standards require lower temperatures than are possible with this method.

farmers use milk cooling devices consisting of metal coils placed directly in the milk cans. An Amish shop near Ashland, Ohio, produces a type of this kind of cooler which operates with circulating cold water. In Lancaster County, Nappanee, and Arthur, Amish dairy farmers comply with Grade A regulations and store their milk in mechanically refrigerated bulk storage tanks.

Milk companies further demand that milk be periodically agitated. The Lancaster Amish accomplish this by running an electric agitator on current obtained from a battery. The battery, in turn, is charged by a generator powered by the diesel engine which runs the other milk equipment. Similar methods are used in the Nappanee and Arthur areas.

Feed Storage

Silos first made their appearance in America in the 1870s and rapidly increased in popularity after 1900. There is no evidence that the Amish ever objected to this new feed storage system. Most Amish, however, use concrete silos and some wooden-stave structures rather than the newer, airtight steel silos (Harvestore type). These new silos need to be unloaded with sophisticated equipment that usually requires electrical power, although a few Amish dairymen have developed hydraulic systems to accomplish the task.

The Amish prefer narrow silos because a whole layer can be shoveled off at each feeding, thus limiting exposure to the air, which causes spoilage.

Often, Amish farmers buy old concrete silos from farmers who no longer want them. These are disassembled and rebuilt on Amish farms. Since many of these silos were meant for much larger dairy operations than those the Amish normally have, they are sometimes made into two Amish silos.

Most modern dairy farmers have mechanical silo unloaders which convey the ensilage from the bottom of the silo. Amish farmers, by contrast, must climb up into the silo and shovel down the ensilage from the top. The Amish also do without the automatic feeding apparatus present on many modern dairy farms. These mechanisms require electricity.

Cleaning Methods

Mechanized barn-cleaning systems to dispose of manure are absent on most Amish farms. A few such devices were introduced on Lancaster Amish farms in the 1960s but later were officially disapproved. Today, Lancaster County farmers generally use horses to pull metal devices through the manure trenches. The manure either goes directly into a manure spreader or into a tank which is later pumped or mechanically conveyed into a spreader.

Some Amish farmers have litter carriers running on tracks through the barn, into which manure is hand shoveled. In the Midwest, barns are typically constructed in such a way that the manure spreader can be driven through the middle of the building and loaded directly.

In the Arthur area and a few other places, manure is loaded into the spreader with small tractor-like machines called skid loaders, or "Bobcats." These are equipped with steel wheels that have rubber tread, rather than with pneumatic tires.

24.
How Do You Run a Woodworking Shop Without Electricity?

GORDONVILLE, Pennsylvania—Joe King and his two teenage sons, David and Amos, had finished breakfast and walked to the shop beside their house. Like many other Amish families in Lancaster County, the Kings needed to supplement their farm income. Today they were building gazebos. A man from New Jersey distributed most of these decorative wooden lawn structures.

Joe went to the control panel at the rear of the shop and pressed a button. The diesel engine in the basement erupted with a dull roar, making the floor vibrate. The same engine powered the vacuum pump for the milker, the refrigeration compressor for the milk cooling system, and the compressed air pump that provided water for the farm.

Above the engine was an old planing machine. It was connected to the engine by a rubber belt extending through a hole in the floor. The belt was fixed around a grooved wheel, on the end of a rotating shaft from the engine.

Joe pulled a lever which tightened the belt on the

planer wheel, sending the machine into motion. The planer's roar soon drowned out the sound of the engine.

As Joe placed long boards beneath the rollers on top of the planer, rotating blades caught hold of the wood and gnawed at the bottom. When the board came through the machine, the planed side had a new, smooth surface.

Joe kept feeding two-by-fours into the machine. Five could fit side by side at the same time. David caught each board as it came out and placed it on a stack.

Close by, Amos sawed sections of three-by-three beams to length. The radial-arm saw he used looked much like a regular electric saw, except for the extra mechanism on one side, into which two rubber hoses were attached. These hoses connected to pipes and a hydraulic pump mounted on the engine in the basement.

The pump circulated oil from a large reservoir beside the engine. The rapid movement of the oil powered the machinery.

Joe had just installed the system and was preparing to put in a hydraulic table saw. Hydraulic equipment was expensive, but it was supposed to provide more efficient power than the electric tools many non-Amish used, and with less wear.

After all of the lumber had been planed, David unhooked a hose that was attached to a hand drill on the opposite side of the shop. He attached the hose to a band saw, then turned a knob that looked like a water spigot on the side of the tool. This did not regulate water, but air. The hose connected to a pipe which went to an air compressor, also attached to the diesel engine.

As David cut the boards, Joe rounded off the edges with a router. Like the saw, this tool ran on compressed air, or pneumatic power.

Amos went to a table saw close to where Joe and David were working. He pulled a wooden lever, which tightened a belt in the same manner as on the planer. This was called the line-shaft method of powering tools. A drill press and welder also were attached to the engine in this way. Amos began making angle cuts in a stack of boards.

By the afternoon, the diesel engine had been shut off, but a large reserve of compressed air had built up in the 2,600 gallon tank in back of the shop. Most of the power hand tools in the shop ran on air. There were two kinds of sanders, a hand planer, a circular saw, a reciprocating saw, staplers, hand drills, and power screw drivers. All could be attached by rubber hoses to the various air outlets situated around the shop.

A few of the items were made to be used with air, but most were modified electric tools. Joe and his boys had made some of the modifications themselves.

Amos and David began assembling the gazebos. They worked rapidly with power nailers—pneumatic guns that could shoot a nail the whole way into the wood with one pull of the trigger.

Soon the gazebos would be ready for pickup and shipment on a special trailer to the distributor.

25.
Power For Manufacturing

The Amish insist that the farm is the best place to maintain their distinctive way of life and the ideal environment in which to raise children. In recent years, however, many Amish have had to find non-agricultural work.

Land in many Amish communities has become expensive and hard to obtain. Along with this, it has become increasingly difficult to make a living solely from farming. Many Amish people who do farm find that they must supplement their income from other sources.

Products Made by the Amish

Dozens of cottage industries operated by the Amish provide for the unique needs of their way of life. Buggy-making and associated crafts, harness- and horse-collar making, horse-shoeing, and the manufacturing of horse-drawn farm implements are among enterprises run by members of the Amish community. There are also many Amish woodworking, cabinet-making, and furniture shops.

In some areas Amish operate sawmill and pallet shops. The construction of utility buildings and recreational shelters such as gazebos and pavilions, primarily for non-Amish people, is a thriving industry. Numerous Amish shops specialize in repairing farm equipment or the gas and diesel engines used on Amish farms. Amish shops manufacture such products as gasoline lamps, wood-burning stoves, kerosene stoves, and water heaters. There are also Amish-run machine shops and foundries which make parts for the machines and appliances used by the Old Order community.

All of these shops and businesses are operated without electricity. This does not mean, however, that they are extremely limited in the kinds of tools they can use. Nearly any type of tool can be adapted to one of the Amish-sanctioned power sources.

Line Shaft, Pneumatic, and Hydraulic Systems

The simplest and oldest method of powering tools and machines is the line shaft. This consists of a rotating shaft connected to a gasoline or diesel engine. The shaft may be attached directly to a machine, but it is more common for drive belts to run from the line shaft to the machine. This system can only be

The blacksmith, or far-rier, is one of many tradesmen who cater to the unique needs of the Amish community.

Modern woodworking equipment is used in many Amish shops, but it is powered hydraulically (like this saw) or by compressed air.

used with larger, stationary machines, such as table saws, drill presses, planers, welders, lathes, and harness-stitchers.

The pneumatic and hydraulic systems used in many Amish shops are more versatile than the line shaft. In a pneumatic system, large tanks are filled with compressed air by engine-powered compressors. Air is piped to various parts of the shop, and hoses for individual tools are plugged into sockets in the air pipe.

Many tools are made especially for compressed air, including circular saws, grinders, and drills. Nearly any other kind of electric hand tool can be converted to pneumatic power by replacing the electrical mechanism with an air motor.

Hydraulic systems work in a similar way to pneumatic ones, except that oil is circulated through pipes and hoses. A special pump powered by an engine creates a rapid flow of oil that motivates the tools. Like the line shaft, hydraulic power is usually reserved for larger machines. An Amish feed mill near Arthur, Illinois, is run entirely with a hydraulic system powered by a Caterpillar diesel engine.

Gasoline Engines and Electric Generators

Portable equipment is sometimes powered by gasoline engines. Most Amish allow chain saws; among some groups who don't, portable motorized circular saws are an acceptable substitute.

Until the 1970s, gas-powered portable hand saws were available commercially. After these were taken off the market, Ervin Hochstetler of the Amish community at Aylmer, Ontario, devised a way to attach a chain saw motor to an electric circular saw. Hochstetler now has a business producing and selling these saws.

This lathe is turned by a small gasoline engine. More typically, a larger engine turns a line shaft, which operates several machines through the use of belts.

In a few Amish communities, electric generators powered by engines are used to provide power for shop tools. Any kind of electric tool can be used in this way. In many communities, portable electric generators are allowed for carpenter crews working on location.

The most conservative Amish communities allow only the line shaft for powering shop tools. In their view, the other methods are too much like electric power.

The Amish in southern Adams County, Indiana, are among the few that do not allow engines even for shop tools. Some animal-powered devices are still used there.

Those Amish who use pneumatic and hydraulic power, or even electric generators, see these methods as quite different from obtaining electricity from public utilities. The power produced in these ways is from individual plants, the moderate Amish point out, and not obtained from a connection with the world. The difference, however, is more symbolic than functional.

26.
Mennonite and Brethren Practices

In addition to the Old Order Amish, several related groups restrict technology for religious reasons. The largest of these groups are the Old Order Mennonites.

These Mennonite fellowships began in the 19th century, when both the Amish and the Mennonite Church experienced major divisions. The more progressive Amish eventually joined the Mennonite Church and adopted modern technology. Several Mennonite groups, on the other hand, withdrew from the Mennonite Church and formed Old Order fellowships.

Pike Mennonites

The oldest and most conservative of the Old Order Mennonites are the Pike Mennonites (named for the Pike meetinghouse in Lancaster County, Pennsylvania). The Pike groups began in 1845 when Jacob Stauffer withdrew from the Lancaster Conference of the Mennonite Church.

During the 20th century, the Pike group has divided several times. The largest of the resulting fellowships is called the Stauffer Mennonite Church. Most of the Stauffers live in Lancaster and Snyder counties in Pennsylvania, but there are churches in Maryland, Missouri, and Kentucky as well. The Stauffers have no cars, electricity, telephones, or self-propelled farm equipment, but they do permit the use of propane gas and engine-powered machinery drawn by horses.

The Weaver Mennonites, who divided from the Stauffers in 1916, allow electricity, telephones, and farming with steel-wheeled tractors. Most of the other groups in the Pike family are more conservative than the Stauffers. The church with the most technological restrictions, the Noah Hoover group, prohibits all use of gasoline engines. Members even use horse power for threshing grain. Founded in Snyder County, Pennsylvania, the Hoover group is now located primarily in Kentucky. In respect to technology, the Hoovers may be more conservative than any Amish group.

A group related to the Hoovers is found in the Central American nation of Belize. Yet another fellowship, the Elam Martin group of Ontario, associates with the Hoovers but does not take as strict a stand on gasoline engines.

Wenger Mennonites

The Wenger, or Groffdale Conference, Mennonites are the largest group of Old Order Mennonites. They stem from an 1893 division in Lancaster Conference.

Technological practices among the Wengers vary widely.

Old Order Mennonites are very similar to the Old Order Amish. These Wenger Mennonites trace their group's beginning to a division that occurred in the Lancaster Mennonite Conference in 1893.

A minority of Old Order Mennonites prohibit the use of tractors for field work. This photo is from a small Wenger Mennonite settlement in Kentucky.

Although the group does not permit ownership of automobiles, non-ordained members are allowed to have electricity and telephones in their homes. However, ordained leaders are not permitted to have high-line power or telephones, and many other members choose to do without these conveniences.

Some traditional families have outside toilets, hand pumps in the kitchen, and kerosene refrigerators, and use cookstoves and heating stoves that burn wood or coal. By contrast, some younger families have modern plumbing and electric ranges and refrigerators, as well as freezers, automatic washers, and dryers and oil-burning furnaces.

Practices often fall somewhere between these two extremes. No Wenger members are permitted to use dishwashers or microwave ovens, and air conditioners are allowed only for people who need them for specific health reasons.

In the main settlement, in Lancaster County, more Wengers own telephones than have electricity. In outlying areas, most people have both in their homes.

Some families that do not tap into electricity from public utilities use engine-powered generators. Wenger members who do not have electricity will typically make use of stationary propane lights fueled from a central tank. Propane is also used for cooking and refrigeration.

While most Mennonites live and dress like modern North Americans, the Old Order groups stress many of the same values as the Amish. Old Order Mennonites typically have large families and live in close-knit communities.

The Wenger church permits self-propelled farm equipment, including tractors, combines, and riding lawn mowers, provided that these have steel wheels. Other implements may have pneumatic tires. Cabs on tractors are discouraged, and members are urged to keep all farm equipment simple and relatively inexpensive.

Woolwich Mennonites

The Woolwich Old Order Mennonite Church of Ontario, formed in 1889, is similar in many ways to the Wenger fellowship. Like the Wengers, Woolwich members are permitted to use electricity but often choose to do without it. Younger families are more likely to have electricity than older ones. Also like Wenger members, many Woolwich families do without indoor toilets, modern plumbing, and water heaters, even though each of these is permitted by the church. The majority of Woolwich households use wood-burning cookstoves, either in addition to gas or electric ranges or exclusively.

Unlike the Wenger church, the Woolwich group forbids the use of telephones in the home, though phones are permitted

The Old Order Mennonite community in Waterloo County, Ontario, is the largest concentration of Plain People in Canada.

in places of business. Woolwich members who do not have businesses often cooperate in having centrally-located community phones that are used by several families.

In addition, the Woolwich group restricts the use of farm implements more than the Wengers do. Self-propelled combines are prohibited, although tractors with pneumatic tires are allowed. Pull-type combines have been accepted, but old-style grain binders and threshing machines continue to be used by many Woolwich farmers. Some farmers cut the grain, then bale it with a hay baler before putting it through a threshing machine.

Old Order Mennonites in Virginia

In 1900, a group in Rockingham County, Virginia, withdrew from the Mennonite Church to form an Old Order fellowship. There are now two Old Order groups in the area.

The larger group, the Showalter Mennonites, allows electricity, telephones, and rubber-tired tractors without cabs. Although many electrical conveniences have been accepted, microwave ovens and air conditioners have not been approved. Most families still use wringer washers and do not have electric clothes dryers. Some younger families have reverted to the use of wood-burning cookstoves.

The smaller group, which divided from the Showalters in 1953, is called the Paul Wenger group (not affiliated with the Wengers in Pennsylvania). This church allows rubber-tired tractors and telephones but does not permit electricity. Members use propane for cooking, refrigerating, and lighting.

Other Old Order Mennonites

The Old Order Mennonites in Elkhart County, Indiana, originated in 1872. Since 1981 there have been two groups of Old Order Mennonites in the state. The larger group is affiliated with the Wenger Mennonites of Pennsylvania. The technological practices of the main Indiana group are nearly identical to those of the Wengers, except that telephones are somewhat less common among the Midwestern group. The smaller Indiana group, known as the Weavers, differs from the Wengers and the other Indiana group in allowing pneumatic rubber tires on tractors.

In addition to these horse-and-buggy groups, there are a number of Old Order Mennonite churches which permit members to drive cars. One such group divided from the Old Order Mennonites in Indiana in 1907 over the use of telephones,

The Reidenbach Old Order Mennonites in Lancaster County do not have modern plumbing and prohibit electricity and telephones.

145

which originally were prohibited by the larger group. The more progressive group, which became known as the Wisler Mennonite Church, eventually adopted not only phones but automobiles. Similar car-driving Old Order groups developed in Pennsylvania (the Horning Mennonites), Ontario (Markham Mennonites), and Virginia (a group affiliated with the Hornings). In Ohio, the great majority of Old Order Mennonites accepted car ownership.

Conversely, a number of groups in addition to those listed above have withdrawn from larger Old Order bodies in order to maintain a more conservative position. One of these is the Reidenbach Mennonite Church of Lancaster County, which withdrew from the Wenger church in 1946.

The Reidenbachs are commonly known as "Thirty-fivers," because that is the number of people who formed the church. The Reidenbachs do not have electricity, telephones, or tractors for field work. Of the four Reidenbach groups that now exist, only one permits the use of propane. "Thirty-fivers" cook with wood, coal, or kerosene. Kerosene-operated refrig-

The Old Order German Baptists in Ohio still use horse-drawn vehicles, as do the related Old Brethren German Baptists in Indiana.

146

erators are permitted, as are motorized washing machines and gasoline pressure lamps. Reidenbach families seldom have indoor bathrooms.

The David Martin Mennonites of Ontario withdrew from the Woolwich church in 1917. For many years they were similar to the Reidenbach Mennonites, but in recent years they have accepted more modern technology. In the 1980s telephones were sanctioned, largely because many of the members had home businesses.

Members of the David Martin group may use propane for cooking and refrigeration, and many have stationary propane light systems. Houses typically have indoor bathrooms. Tractors are prohibited, but members may hire people outside the group to do custom work with modern machinery.

Old Order Brethren

Two groups of German Baptist, or "Dunker," background have retained an Old Order lifestyle. The Old Brethren German Baptists, who live primarily in Indiana, organized in 1913. The Old Order German Baptists, organized in 1921, are found primarily in Ohio.

Both groups divided form the Old German Baptist Church, and both prohibit cars, electricity, and telephones. The Old Order German Baptists permit the use of tractors with pneumatic tires, while the Old Brethren German Baptists farm with horses. The Old Brethren group does use motorized, horse-drawn machinery, such as hay balers.

Among both groups, propane is used for cooking, refrigeration, and heating water, though some families prefer to cook with older methods, such as wood-burning stoves. A few families have centralized propane lighting systems, but most use portable pressurized lamps.

Similar in theology to German Baptist groups, but entirely different in history, are the Old Order River Brethren. One group of Old Order River Brethren, in Franklin County, Pennsylvania, maintains the use of horse-drawn vehicles.

However, this group has allowed the use of electricity, telephones, and modern farm equipment for years.

Old Colony Mennonites

In several Latin American countries, there are large populations of Mennonites who restrict modern technology. These are the Old Colony Mennonites, whose ancestors migrated from south Russia to the province of Manitoba in Canada in the 1870s.

The most conservative Old Colony Mennonites moved from Manitoba and Saskatchewan to Mexico in the 1920s. Forty years later, the most conservative Old Colony members in Mexico moved to Bolivia. Today there are settlements in Belize, Paraguay, and Argentina, as well. The lifestyle of these Old Colony groups is distinct from that of other Latin American Mennonites, who accept modern methods and devices.

In Bolivia, the Old Colony Mennonites live near the city of Santa Cruz in the tropical lowlands. Although electrical service would be available, the Old Colony church allows only

The Old Colony Mennonites in Latin America limit technology, as do the Amish and Old Order Mennonites.

Old Colony Mennonites manufacture their own windmills. Some parts of the mechanism are ingeniously adapted from discarded auto parts.

individual electric generators. These may be used for shop work, such as welding, but are not to power home lighting systems. Kerosene lamps and mantle lamps fueled by small propane tanks are the usual light sources. Propane also is used to run stoves and refrigerators.

Water in this community is usually pumped by windmills, which are made in local shops. Old Colony blacksmiths have become ingenious in adapting salvaged auto parts for use in these and other mechanical devices. It is said that differentials from certain model years of Dodge and Plymouth cars are preferred for use in windmill mechanisms. Other auto parts find a second life in horse-drawn vehicles.

Outdoor toilets are still the norm in the Bolivian Old Order settlements. Water is not piped into the houses, but must be carried in from the outside. Washing machines are powered by gasoline engines.

While horses are still used for transportation, tractors with steel wheels are used for most farm work. Nearly any kind of agricultural implement is permitted.

Old Colony Practices in Mexico

The oldest and largest Old Colony settlement in the world is located in northern Mexico, near the town of Cuauhtemoc in the state of Chihuahua. During the 1980s, many Mennonites in this area left the Old Colony church, and those who stayed modified their traditional practices. (Several smaller Old Colony settlements in Mexico remain like those in Bolivia.)

At Cuauhtemoc, tractors with pneumatic tires are now accepted and the use of pickup trucks has increased rapidly. Pickups are preferred to cars because they are more practical for farmers and are more easily imported from the United States.

As of 1988, members were not allowed to drive motor vehicles into the yards of Old Colony churches, but it was permissible to park at a neighboring farm and walk to church. A few older people continued to use horse-drawn transportation during the week, but vehicles of this sort were a rare sight in town.

Many Old Colony members now receive electricity from public utilities. Those people who do not have electricity use propane for cooking, refrigeration, and lighting. Telephones are not readily available in this part of Mexico, but some people have two-way radios, which are used in much the same manner as phones. Modern kitchens and bathrooms are typical in Old Colony homes in the area.

A Short History of the Amish

The Amish trace their roots to the Anabaptist movement, which began in 1525 in Switzerland and developed separately in Holland a few years later. Most Anabaptists eventually became identified as Mennonites, after a prominent Dutch leader, Menno Simons.

Unlike the Protestant Reformers, the Anabaptists practiced adult, voluntary baptism and separation of church and state. They refused to take a part in war or any other form of violence, and they viewed the literal teachings of the Bible as a guide for all areas of life.

In 1693, a young bishop named Jacob Amman led a group that separated form the Mennonite churches of Switzerland, the Alsace, and the German Palatinate. Amman stressed greater simplicity of life and stricter church discipline than other Mennonites in these regions, and he wished to adopt the Dutch Mennonite practices of feet washing and shunning excommunicated members. Amman's followers became known as Amish.

Following an earlier migration of Mennonites, the Amish sought homes in North America early in the 1700s. They settled in Pennsylvania and pushed on to Ohio, Indiana, and Iowa by the mid-19th century. The westward movement was augmented by a new wave of Amish immigrants directly from Europe.

During the second half of the 19th century, the more progressive Amish in the New World parted with the conserva-

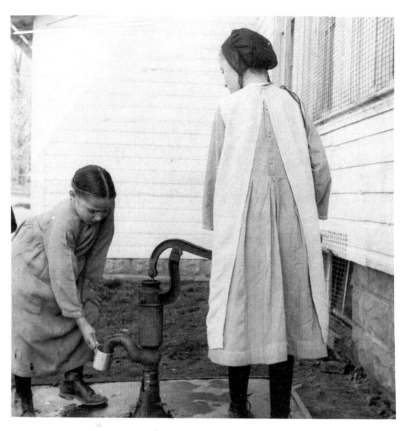

*The Old Order Amish are not against change, but try to carefully deter-
mine which changes might adversely affect their church and community.*

tives. Like those Amish who had remained in Europe, the pro-
gressives eventually merged with the Mennonites.

The conservatives, who became known as Old Order
Amish, have tried to control cultural and technological influences from the larger society. They believe that the church,
guided by the Bible, is responsible to institute guidelines for
how its members act in all areas of life.

The Amish believe it is very important for Christians to be
separate from the world, both inwardly and outwardly. This is
reflected in their dress, their form of worship, their language,
and their use of technology.

Bibliography

The Amish and Related Groups

Bringing the Airtight Revolution into the Kitchen. Aylmer, Ontario: Suppertime Stoves, n.d.

"The Choice of Two Evils," *Family Life* (Feb. 1976), 10-13. A story about why Amish don't have telephones.

Cronk, Sandra. *Gelassenheit: The Rites of the Redemptive Process in Old Order Amish and Old Order Mennonite Communities*. Ph.D. Dissertation, University of Chicago, 1977.

Dyck, Cornelius (ed.). *An Introduction to Mennonite History*. Scottdale, Pennsylvania: Herald Press, 1993.

Fisher, Gideon. *Farm Life and Its Changes*. Gordonville, Pennsylvania: Pequea Publishers, 1978.

Gallagher, Thomas Edward, Jr. *Clinging to the Past or Preparing for the Future? The Structure of Selective Modernization Among the Old Order Amish of Lancaster County, Pennsylvania*. Ph.D. Dissertation, Temple University, 1981.

Glick, Ivan J. "Farm Sale," *The Draft Horse Journal*. (Fall 1982), 10-13.

Good, Merle. *Who Are the Amish?* Intercourse, Pennsylvania: Good Books, 1999.

Good, Merle and Phyllis. *Twenty Most Asked Questions about the Amish and Mennonites*. Intercourse, Pennsylvania: Good Books, 1995.

Horst, Isaac R. *Separate and Peculiar*. Mt. Forest, Ontario: Isaac R. Horst, 1979.

Hostetler, John A. *Amish Society*. Baltimore: Johns Hopkins University Press, 1993.

Huntington, Gertrude Enders. *Dove at the Window: A Study of an Old Order Amish Community in Ohio*. Ph.D. Dissertation. Yale University, 1957.

Johnson, Warren A., Victor Stoltzfus and Peter Craumer. "Energy Conservation in Amish Agriculture," *Science*, Vol. 198 (Oct. 1977), 373-378.

Kline, David. "No-Till Farming and Its Threat to the Amish Community," *Festival Quarterly*, Vol. 13, No. 2 (Fall 1986), 7-10.

Kollmorgen, Walter M. *Culture of a Contemporary Rural Community: The Old Order Amish of Lancaster County, Pennsylvania.* Washington, D.C.: U.S. Department of Agriculture, Rural Life Studies, 1942.

Kraybill, Donald B. *The Riddle of Amish Culture.* Baltimore: Johns Hopkins University Press, 1988.

"The Leacock Lamp," *The Coleman Lite*, No. 7 (April 1984), 1-2.

Logsdon, Gene. "Produce Acres, A Horse-Powered Vegetable Farm," *The Draft Horse Journal*, Vol. 24, No. 4 (Winter 1987-1988), 5-14.

The Mennonite Encyclopedia. Scottdale, Pennsylvania: Herald Press, 1959, 1972.

Nordell, Eric. "Lancaster Forecarts," *Small Farmer's Journal*, Vol. 12, No. 3 (Summer 1988), 56-59.

Scott, Stephen E. *Plain Buggies.* Intercourse, Pennsylvania: Good Books, 1998.

Stoll, Elmo. *One-Way Street.* Aylmer, Ontario: Pathway Publishers, 1972.

Stoll, Joseph. "When the Old-Fashioned Was New-Fangled," *Young Companion* (August 1988), 27-32.

Umble, John (ed.). "Memoirs of an Amish Bishop," *Mennonite Quarterly Review*, XXII (April 1948), 94-116.

Wagler, David L. *Are All Things Lawful?* Aylmer, Ontario: Pathway Publishers, n.d.

_____. "The Oldest Form of Energy," *Family Life* (January 1985), 38 ff.

Wagler, David S. *History and Change of the Amish Community of Reno County, Kansas.* Unpublished paper. Bethel College, North Newton, Kansas, 1968.

"Welcome to the World of New 1983 Horse Machinery," *The Draft Horse Journal* (Autumn 1983), 7-20.

General Technological History

Anderson, Oscar Edward, Jr. *Refrigeration in America: A History of a New Technology and Its Impact.* Princeton, New Jersey: Princeton University Press, 1953. Reissued, Port Washington, New York: Kennikat Press, 1972.

Bobrowski, Robert George. *Rediscovering the Woodburning Cookstove.* Old Greenwich, Connecticut: Chatham Press, 1976.

A Brief History of the Origin and Use of Coleman Lamps and Lanterns. Wichita, Kansas: The Coleman Company, 1980.

Courter, J. W. *Aladdin—The Magic Name in Lamps.* Simpson, Illinois, J. W. Courter, 1971.

Cowan, Ruth Schwartz. *More Work for Mother: The Ironies of Household Technology from the Open Hearth to Microwave.* New York: Basic Books, 1983.

DeBono, Edward (ed.). *Eureka, An Illustrated History of Inventions from the Wheel to the Computer.* New York: Holt-Rinehart, 1974.

Ebendorf, Herbert W. *The Gasoline Self-Heating Iron.* Wichita, Kansas: The Coleman Company, n.d.

_____. *Gas from Gasoline.* Wichita, Kansas: The Coleman Company, 1972. A history of gasoline pressure lamps.

Franklin, Linda Campbell. *From Hearth to Cookstove.* Florence, Alabama: House of Collectibles, 1976.

Giedon, Siegfried. *Mechanization Takes Command.* New York: Oxford University Press, 1948. Reprinted, New York: W.W. Norton, 1969.

Glissman, A. H. *The Evolution of the Sad Iron.* Oceanside, California: M.B. Printing, 1970.

Lantz, Louise K. *Old American Kitchenware 1725-1925.* Hanover, Pennsylvania: Everybody's Press, 1970.

Lifshey, Earl. *The Housewares Story.* Chicago: National Housewares Manufacturing Association, 1973.

Matson, Tim. *Alternative Light Styles.* Woodstock, Vermont: Countryman Press, 1984.

Maytag Wringer Washers 1907-1983. Newton, Iowa: The Maytag Company, n.d.

Mercer, Henry C. (edited by Horace M. Mann and Joseph Sanford). *The Bible in Iron: Pictorial Stove and Stoveplates of the Pennsylvania Germans.* Doylestown, Pennsylvania: Bucks County Historical Society, 1961.

Panati, Charles. *Extraordinary Origins of Everyday Things.* New York: Harper and Row, 1987.

Pierce, Josephine H. *Fire on the Hearth: The Evolution and Romance of the Heating Stove.* Springfield, Massachusetts: Pond-Ekberg, 1951.

Russell, Loris S. *A Heritage of Light.* Toronto: University of Toronto Press, 1968.

_____. *Handy Things To Have Around the House.* Toronto: McGraw Hill-Ryerson, 1979.

Strasser, Susan. *Never Done: A History of American Housework.* New York: Pantheon, 1982.

Thuro, Catherine M. V. *Oil Lamps: The Kerosene Era in North America.* Des Moines, Iowa: Wallace Homestead, 1976.

Worthington, William E., Jr. *Beyond the City Lights: American Domestic Gas Lighting Systems.* Washington, D.C.: The Smithsonian Institution, 1985.

Technology On the Farm

Baker, T. Lindsay. *A Field Guide to American Windmills.* Norman, Oklahoma: University of Oklahoma Press, 1985.

Berry, Wendell. *The Unsettling of America.* San Francisco: The Sierra Club, 1977.

Cummins, C. Lyle. *Internal Fire: The Internal Combustion Engine 1673-1900.* Lake Oswego, Oregon: Carnot Press, 1976.

Danhof, Clarence. *Change in Agriculture, The Northern U.S. 1820-1870.* Cambridge, Massachusetts: Harvard University Press, 1969.

Fletcher, Stevenson Whitcomb. *Pennsylvania Agriculture and Country Life* (two volumes). Harrisburg, Pennsylvania: Pennsylvania Historical and Museum Commission, 1955.

Hurt, R. Douglas. *American Farm Tools.* Manhattan, Kansas: Sunflower University Press, 1982.

Johnson, Paul C. *Farm Power in the Making of America.* Des Moines, Iowa: Wallace Homestead, 1978.

_____. *Farm Inventions in the Making of America.* Des Moines, Iowa: Wallace Homestead, 1976.

McKinley, Marvin. *Wheels of Farm Progress.* St. Joseph, Michigan: American Society of Agricultural Engineers, 1980.

Macmillan, Don and Russel Jones. *John Deere Tractors and Equipment, Volume I 1837-1959.* St. Joseph, Michigan: American Society of Agricultural Engineers, 1988.

Miller, Lynn R. *Work Horse Handbook.* Reedsport, Oregon: Mill Press, 1981.

Mills, Robert K. *Implement and Tractor: One Hundred Years of Farm Equipment.* Overland Park, Kansas: Intertech, 1986.

Power to Produce, The Yearbook of Agriculture 1960. Washington, D.C.: U.S. Department of Agriculture, 1960.

Quick, Graeme and Wesley Buchele. *The Grain Harvester.* St. Joseph, Michigan: American Society of Agricultural Engineers, 1978.

Rosenberg, S. H. (ed.), *Rural America a Century Ago.* St. Joseph, Michigan: American Society of Agricultural Engineers, 1976.

Schlebecker, John T. *Whereby We Thrive, A History of American Farming 1607-1972.* Ames, Iowa: Iowa State University, 1975.

Telleen, Marice. *The Draft Horse Primer.* Emmaus, Pennsylvania: Rodale Press, 1977.

Wendel, C. H. *American Gasoline Engines Since 1872.* Sarasota, Florida: Crestline Publishing, 1983.

_____. *One Hundred Fifty Years of International Harvester.* Sarasota, Florida: Crestline Publishing, 1981.

About the Authors

Stephen Scott became interested in the Plain People while a teenager in southwestern Ohio. He moved to Lancaster County, Pennsylvania, in 1969 and later became a member of the Old Order River Brethren.

His books include *Plain Buggies: Amish, Mennonite, and Brethren Horse-Drawn Transportation, Why Do They Dress That Way?* and *The Amish Wedding and Other Special Occasions of the Old Order Communities.* He and his wife, Harriet, have three children and live near Columbia, Pennsylvania.

Kenneth Pellman and his wife, Rachel, are co-authors of *The World of Amish Quilts, A Treasury of Amish Quilts,* and *A Treasury of Mennonite Quilts.*

The Pellmans live near Lancaster, Pennsylvania, with their two sons.